Creative
Dimensions
of Suffering

Creative
Dimensions
of Suffering

A-M. Ghadirian, M.D.

Bahá'í
PUBLISHING
Wilmette, Illinois

Bahá'í Publishing
415 Linden Avenue, Wilmette, Illinois 60091-2844

Copyright © 2009 by the National Spiritual Assembly
of the Bahá'ís of the United States

All rights reserved. Published 2009
Printed in the United States of America on acid-free paper ∞

12   11   10   4   3   2

Library of Congress Cataloging-in-Publication Data

Ghadirian, A–M (Abdu'l-Missagh)
  Creative dimensions of suffering / A–M Ghadirian.
      p. cm.
  Includes bibliographical references and index.
  ISBN 978-1-931847-60-5
  1. Suffering. 2. Creative ability. I. Title.

  BF789.S8G45 2009
  204'.42—dc22

                                        2009003026

Cover design by Robert A. Reddy
Book design by Suni D. Hannan

Acknowledgments

Connecting the concepts of suffering and creativity has been a formidable challenge. There are a number of individuals to whom I am grateful for their assistance in completing this book. I am immensely appreciative of Dr. Merryl Hammond's invaluable review, suggestions, and editing. Likewise, I am thankful to Christopher Martin and Terry Cassiday for their thoughtful comments and editing. My sincere thanks go to Dr. Bruce L. Miller for his copyright permission to publish two works of art in this book. I would also like to thank Claire Gougeon and Marie-Claire Rioux for their diligent secretarial assistance. As exploration of the subject of this book required extensive research in the appropriate literature, I was aided by librarian Giovanna Badia and her assistant Anne-Marie Hince at the McGill University Health Centre libraries. Their efficiency and timely support were much appreciated. My deep gratitude also goes to my dear wife Marilyn whose insightful comments, assistance in typing and editing, and loving support sustained me in completing this work.

Contents

Contents

Contents

Introduction

The relationship between the creative process and suffering has been a subject of interest for centuries, and even since the time of Aristotle, philosophers and behavioral scientists have developed many theories on the nature of this relationship. During the past few decades, research on the characteristics of creativity in relation to psychosocial life crises has led to remarkable breakthroughs. Nevertheless, the neuropsychological interaction between creativity and suffering remains an enigma, and even finding clear-cut definitions for *creativity* and *suffering* has posed challenges to many researchers.

Suffering is a universal experience. When suffering occurs, people begin to raise questions about the purpose of life and their ultimate destiny. They begin to search for meaning in the universe around them. The founders of the world's religions have addressed the problem of suffering in two ways. First, they have tried to place the issue of human pain and suffering in the larger context of the universe and our understanding of it. Second, they have shown ways to overcome and transcend human suffering through faith, spirituality, and appropriate actions.[1]

In contrast, the study of science has responded differently to suffering. Unlike religion, science explores the nature and the characteristics of suffering, and it has invented ways to measure and quantify the effect of pain on the body and mind. Despite the explanations and theories of science regarding suffering, however, the elucidation of the purpose and meaning of pain and adversity remains largely within the domain of religion.

When we bring up questions of how suffering and creativity are interrelated, the answers become even more elusive. Traditionally, suffering has been perceived as a morbid experience, a black hole of human existence that always imparts fear and anxiety. If we explore this dark continent called *suffering*, however, we often find bright sides of it that have been the direct or indirect cause of great achievements in society. Indeed, many

1

historical figures who endured great suffering were able to find a purpose to their adversity, and they emerged victorious over their hardships.

How is this possible? Why do some people succeed at overcoming their suffering while others succumb and are crushed by calamity and misery? Is there a certain group of people who are more likely than others to have their creative potential released during or after ordeals involving suffering? Is there any pathway or mechanism that allows creativity to develop during adversity? Do genes or environment play a special role in overcoming adversity, or is there a unique relationship between spirituality and creativity?

We don't have answers for all of these intriguing questions, but we will explore many of them in this book. What is suffering for one person may be a normal existential experience for someone else, and what is perceived as valuable creative work in one culture may be viewed as a boring exercise in another. Among the theoretical models of creativity, one model defines a creative person as a gifted and chosen individual who is inspired by his or her unique mind and intellect. In another model, creativity is perceived as the product of an altered state of consciousness in which regression into a preconscious state is translated into the language of art or other creative experiences. Therefore, the understanding and appreciation of creativity varies from culture to culture and from model to model. As a result, researchers have encountered many difficulties in formulating a universal model for the study of creativity. This lack of consensus, in turn, often confounds our understanding of the relationship between creativity and mental or physical suffering.

Another complication is the scarcity of research literature on spirituality and suffering in relation to creativity. However, spiritual writings may provide new insights on the interplay between suffering and faith, both of which are intertwined with the creative process. This relationship has a measurable impact on personal growth and transformation, and studying it provides valuable understanding of the relationship between crisis and victory in our personal lives and in our communities.

This book is not only about the moaning and groaning of life crises and ordeals, nor is it intended to romanticize suffering. It is a celebration of the achievements of countless men and women who have suffered in different ways. Many struggled and passed through their tragedy with courage and perseverance. Many others never saw the result of their struggle during their own lifetime, and some died in poverty and despair. But the generations who followed them discovered the genius of their contribution and celebrated their achievements with gratitude. Although research has found a trend suggesting that depression and bipolar disorder are more prevalent in creative populations such as poets, writers and artists, this should not be generalized to assume that all creative individuals are predisposed to such afflictions. In fact, more studies are needed to validate these findings.

The book is divided into eleven chapters, and each explores a specific subject related to the main theme of the relationship between creativity and suffering. To explain this relationship, the author has drawn on personal knowledge and experience as well as extensive research in literature to examine theories about the interplay between suffering, resilience, and creativity. He has explored the lives of artists, writers, poets, scientists, and ordinary individuals who have risen above their own suffering and left behind a legacy of unique and amazing experiences. Their encounters with and victory over adversity testify to the presence of another force, beyond a human being's physical or mental capability, that reinforces the individual during periods of intense suffering.

It is the author's hope that the insights and anecdotes from the experiences of various gifted individuals who turned their life crises into creative developments will serve as an inspiration to everyone who struggles daily with adversity.

Abdu'l-Missagh Ghadirian
February 2009

1

Understanding Suffering

"Suffering ceases to be suffering in some way at the moment it finds a meaning such as the meaning of sacrifice."

— *Viktor Frankl*

Suffering and sufferance stem from the Latin word *sufferentia,* meaning *endurance.* The word also refers to the bearing of pain, affliction, or misery. Furthermore, "suffer" means to permit, to tolerate, or to be subjected to pain, grief, distress, or death. Suffering is defined as "the experience of organisms in situations that involve physical and mental pain, usually attended by a sense of loss, frustration, and vulnerability to adverse effects." In the Western world, suffering has a negative connotation that implies morbidity, abnormality, or sickness. However, suffering can also carry many benefits and is at times a blessing in disguise. Scientist Hans Selye remarked that stress is like the spice of life—without this spice, life loses its excitement and can be boring.[1]

SUFFERING AND ITS MEANING

According to Eric Cassell, "suffering occurs when an impending destruction of the person is perceived; it continues until the threat of disintegration has passed or until the integrity of the person can be restored in some other manner . . . suffering extends beyond the physical. Most generally, suffering can be defined as the state of severe distress associated with events that threaten the intactness of the person." He further elaborates that although pain and suffering are closely related to one another, they are fundamentally different, as the greatest pain does not necessarily cause the greatest suffering. For example, although the pain of childbirth can be extremely severe for a woman in labor, the end result—the birth of a child—is a rewarding experience for the new mother.[2]

MATERIAL VERSUS SPIRITUAL SUFFERING

According to the Bahá'í writings, suffering can be divided into two types—material and spiritual. 'Abdu'l-Bahá* writes, "There is no human being untouched by these two influences [joy and pain]; but all the sorrow and the grief that exist come from the world of matter—the spiritual world bestows only the joy!"[3] Some people believe that suffering in the path of God is more acceptable than leading a life of ease and comfort, as suffering can bring one closer to God. Such people often have a deep understanding of the meaning and purpose of life and believe in the spiritual nature of a human being and that one's spiritual evolution continues beyond this world. Because of these beliefs, they are more likely to face death with a sense of contentment as compared to those who perceive their life as merely a physical existence. The former often show resilience in the face of suffering, while the latter often fear suffering.

Imprisoned for four years in a hard labor camp for participating in what was perceived to be anti-government activities, Dostoyevsky viewed the suffering associated with the acceptance of "a harsh punishment as an atonement for his crime and as a purification of his conscience. This frame of mind led him to a heightened respect for the established order of society in Russia and to an increased devotion to the teachings of Christ . . . he even began to perceive wonderful qualities in his fellow convicts . . . these 'common people' of his native land. In short, prison defined and deepened his creative process, taught him the doctrine of salvation by suffering, and provided him with rich material for a continued analysis of the souls of the insulted and injured."[4]

The more we are attached (excessively) to the material world of existence, the more we will experience pain and distress should we be separated from it. In fact, we can conclude that the more the society around us encourages indulgence in pleasure, the more we are in danger of losing sight of our true self and inner reality.

PAIN AND SUFFERING

Although the words *pain* and *suffering* are often used interchangeably, nevertheless they represent two distinct concepts, according to Eric Cassell.

---

* Son of Bahá'u'lláh, the Prophet-Founder of the Bahá'í Faith. He became the head of the Faith after Bahá'u'lláh's passing.

Suffering, he notes, is usually perceived as a psychological experience, while pain is quite often referred to as a physical experience. Cassell believes that patients may tolerate severe pain and not consider it *suffering* if they know that the pain is controllable and will end. In contrast, he points out that a minor pain may become the source of suffering if that pain stems from a dire and uncontrollable cause such as cancer. In such circumstances the feeling of helplessness and hopelessness may intensify suffering.[5]

To bolster his argument, Cassell gives the following example: "a patient reported that when she believed the pain in her leg was sciatica, she could control it with small doses of codeine, but when she discovered that it was due to the spread of a malignant disease, much greater amounts of medication were required for relief." Cassell therefore concluded that suffering from pain is frequently reported when people feel that their pain is out of control, overwhelming, originating from an unknown source, or chronic.[6]

H. G. Koenig points out that psychological pain is different from physical pain, as psychological pain is usually the result of an insult to the integrity and innate state of self while physical pain affects the body only. However, psychological pain can also result from a disabling physical pain as well, and depression is often an emotional expression of this form of pain. For example, depressed patients have greater propensity to pain, and approximately 50 percent of patients with serious depression also suffer from chronic pain.[7]

WHY DO WE SUFFER?

Human beings are not perfect. Life in this world is a path toward perfection on which individuals are challenged to strive for excellence in preparation for the next world. Thus suffering is unavoidable and plays a role in personal growth and learning how to overcome weaknesses. The experience of suffering can have ennobling effects that make us reflect on the deeper meaning of our existence. Suffering can be physical, psychological, or spiritual, but regardless of the source, it always has meaning. If sorrow and suffering were to vanish completely during one's life, what kind of living would that be? Would it be a happier life? What would we be comparing happiness to? In such a case, happiness and pleasure would lose their meaning. Imagine that life in this world were eternal and that there were no death. What would life be like? In the world of nature, we see contrasts and paradoxes that help us appreciate each side by comparison. Examples of these contrasts are summer and winter, wealth and poverty, high mountains and deep valleys. If we were never to see a dark night, how could we appreciate the beauty of daylight? The idea is not to seek out suffering; it is rather to acknowledge and understand it and accept the fact that suffering is a natural part of life in spite of our efforts to avoid it.

Some people cannot accept unhappiness and resort to artificial means to try to find happiness. In a consumer society in which people are overindulged and overmedicated to restore their comfort levels, feeling unhappy may lead some people to resort to alcohol or stimulants. There are drugs that are called drugs of "lifestyle." These are designed and marketed to respond to changes in lifestyle and discontentment. Science has invented a variety of drugs to improve our lifestyle. For example, there are drugs to stop smoking, to reduce weight, to prevent hair loss, to enhance athletes' performance, to prevent gambling or drug addiction, or to increase sexual functioning. We can be reconstructed from nose to toes to improve our appearance. Such phenomena show how much we rely on external interventions to remedy our internal emptiness and discontentment.

The results of a survey of 644 Harvard University alumni showed that 40 percent of the alumni were not content with their life, despite an academic degree from a world-class university and an average annual income of $300,000.[8] Clearly, material prosperity is not by itself the key to enduring contentment.

FINDING MEANING IN SUFFERING

Finding a meaning and purpose in life crises and adversity may not eradicate pain—regardless of whether the pain is physical or psychological—but some research shows that having a sense of meaning will mitigate the impact of pain on a person and will make it more bearable. Viktor Frankl, a Viennese psychiatrist who survived the Auschwitz concentration camp, wrote the following account after his release from the camp.

One day an elderly general practitioner came to Dr. Frankl's office for help. The man had been very depressed since the loss of his beloved wife two years earlier. He listened to this patient and wondered what solution he could offer. He couldn't revive the patient's wife, nor could he change the man's fate. Thus Dr. Frankl decided to confront him with a question. He asked the elderly man, "What would have happened, Doctor, if you had died first and your wife would have had to survive you?" His patient replied, "Oh, for her this would have been terrible; how she would have suffered!" Then Dr. Frankl said, "You see, Doctor, such a suffering has been spared her, and it is you who have spared her this suffering; now you have to pay for it by surviving and mourning her." The patient (doctor) appeared to be comforted and content with that remark and calmly left the office. In that situation, the patient became conscious of the meaning of the loss, and his insight alleviated his anguish and suffering.[9]

We can conclude, based on this account, that a relationship appears to exist between suffering and meaninglessness in life. Patients nearing the end of life in palliative care units, for example, very often lose hope. Not all patients who suffer from a loss of hope also suffer from depression, although hopelessness and depression are interrelated. A loss of hope in a group of terminally ill patients, however, can have a different meaning. At the terminal stage of an illness, patients are confronted with many and often troubling thoughts and questions. Some of these questions are essentially spiritual in nature, such as what will happen to them after death, whether there is another world beyond this world, whether they will have any awareness of this world after death, or whether they will be able to see their loved ones in the next world. One common question that patients have at this stage is what the purpose and meaning of physical existence are and whether there is any hope for the future.

Sometimes the sense of despair and loss of hope reach such a degree that some patients may want to hasten their death. By restoring a sense of meaning and purpose in life, we can help patients to regain a sense of hope and faith and to accept suffering or at least to mitigate the intensity of their despair and unhappiness. Victor Frankl has written, "Man is not destroyed by suffering: he is destroyed by suffering without meaning," and Shoghi Effendi* has written, "Suffering is both a reminder and a guide . . . But it is not always easy to find the secret of that wisdom.

---

* The Guardian of the Bahá'í Faith who headed the Faith after the passing of 'Abdu'l-Bahá.

It is sometimes only when all our suffering has passed that we become aware of its usefulness."[10] Thus, although it is important to understand the meaning of suffering, we may not be able at times to have a clear realization of its purpose and wisdom.

HEALING, SPIRITUALITY, AND SUFFERING

A number of researchers who work with patients in palliative care units or hospices and related environments have been exploring meaning-centered care. According to their report, helping terminal patients find meaning in life can have a remedial effect on their sense of hopelessness. Breitbart and colleagues were inspired by Viktor Frankl's book *Man's Search for Meaning* when developing their own model of meaning-centered care. The eight-week course they created is based on cognitive psychotherapy but also focuses on the meaning of life. Patients are asked questions in the form of meaning-centered exercises, such as remembering or elaborating on certain creative activities they have done in their lives such as art, or work. The facilitators of the course then try to establish with their patients an understanding of the meaning of life through the patients' activities.[11]

Many patients gain strength and find comfort when turning to God and reciting prayers for healing and relief from suffering. The recitation of prayers also helps some patients reflect on the purpose of life and their relationship with their Creator. Prayer has a mystic potency of spiritual proportion that connects us to the source of our being, gives meaning and hope to our lives, and assists us to rely on our faith. It reinforces the fact that human life is essentially a spiritual journey and that birth and death are stages of our spiritual transformation and evolution as human beings. The Bahá'í writings and other religious scriptures emphasize the importance of prayer and meditation for the well-being of humanity.

Patients may vary in their perception of life and its meaning in relation to the healing process. For example, Mount et al. related anecdotes of two patients suffering from cancer. They stated that one person with a positive mindset may die and be healed emotionally while another person who has a negative mindset may continue to live but not experience the same kind of emotional healing. The following are two such cases.[12]

The first case involved a thirty-year-old man who was suffering from severe metastatic cancer near the end of life. One day he said good-bye to his physician and added, "This last year has been the best of my life." His doctor was surprised by this statement and asked how it was possible that a year filled with agony could be considered the best of his life. The patient replied that it was because he had experienced a new awareness of the spiritual aspect of his existence.

The second case concerned a widow in her seventies with breast carcinoma that had metastasized to her bone and caused her much pain. The pain did not respond to analgesics, including morphine, and her physician was puzzled by her plight and one day asked her, "When were you last well?" The patient inquired if he was referring to her physical pain, and he replied, "No, I mean in yourself." She responded, "Doctor, I have never been well a day in my life." She then added, "I've been sick in mind and spirit every day of my life." She continued in anguish and pain until she died a few days later. Analysis of these cases showed that the first patient reached the stage of healing while approaching death but that the second patient was neither physically cured nor holistically healed. If we define healing as an experience that encompasses the whole person, we can say that these two cases differed from each other significantly even though both of them were suffering from cancer.

2

Dimensions in Creativity

"Art is a step in the known toward the unknown."

—Khalil Gibran

Creativity and change are interrelated and are like two sides of the same coin. Creativity brings change, and change may kindle creative development. Creativity is a phenomenon characterized by originality, expressiveness, and imaginative productivity. It brings about a change. Change is an essential expression of creativity and may be associated with joy or pain. One Web site notes that "being creative is seeing the same thing as everybody else, but thinking of something different" and that "creativity involves the translation of our unique gifts, talents and vision into an external reality that is new and useful."[1]

DEFINITION OF CREATIVITY

Different definitions exist for the terms *creative, creativity,* and *creation. Webster's Dictionary* defines creativity as "creative ability, artistic or intellectual inventiveness." Crutch et al. state that visual art, specifically, is "in essence a creative activity concerned with the generation of new designs and ideas. Acts of creation such as paintings capture our imagination, not simply because we are able to explore their nature, but also because they reflect the nature of their creator. It is this relation that makes the examination of artistic and creative talent in the context of illness so revealing." According to Richards and Kinney, Einstein emphasized the importance of creative persons' having access to their dreams, which in Freudian terms would be primary process thinking.[2]

TYPES OF CREATIVITY

Now that we have defined creativity, we can start to look at whether creativity is a single process or whether it can be divided into different "types." For example, Richards and Kinney distinguish between two types

13

of creativity: eminent and everyday creativity. According to these two authors, eminent creativity requires originality with social recognition, while everyday creativity is defined as an adaptive capacity and requires originality and adaptation to reality. Richards and Kinney in another place have also defined two levels of creativity: major and minor. According to them, major creativity requires a significant change in an individual's own conceptual framework. For example, Pasteur's germ theory of disease was a major rethinking of the origins of infections. When one uses minor creativity, however, one applies existing strategies to new tasks. These authors recognize that creativity may be limited to one area and may not necessarily apply to all areas of life.[3]

In contrast to Richards, and Kinney's view, author Maureen Neihart defines creativity as a bridge between rational and irrational thoughts. She writes, "Since the time of the Greek philosophers, those who wrote about the creative process emphasized that creativity involves a regression to more primitive mental processes, that to be creative requires a willingness to cross and re-cross the lines between rational and irrational thoughts."[4] What Neihart refers to as creativity probably relates to a narrow field of creativity because it does not explain creativity that is purely based on rational thinking. For example, the relativity theory of Einstein was a genuinely creative accomplishment that resulted in new conceptual thinking and was entirely based on a rational search after new truth. Therefore the idea that inspiration requires regression and penetration into primitive and irrational mental processes in order to access unconscious thoughts does not seem to apply to all creative processes. This understanding of creativity is useful because it means that creativity can be found in all professions and not just those that focus on art. The fields of medicine and psychology, for example, are prime examples of professions that can benefit from harnessing the healing powers of creative expression. When Plato writes that creativity is a "divine madness . . . a gift from the gods" or Aristotle states, "No great genius was without a mixture of insanity," they seem to indicate the unknown dimension of creativity that modern science is able to explore and explain. Creativity is not limited to creating art or discovering new scientific findings. It can have much broader implications. For example, a firefighter who finds a way to save an infant from a raging house fire when all normal avenues of rescue are blocked has engaged in a noble act of creativity. Likewise, a caretaker who assists a disabled or paralyzed person to discover ways to help himself or herself is rendering a creative service.

H. Edward Tryk takes a different approach from Neihart or Richards and Kinney. Tryk defines creativity based on its particular characteristics for psychological measurement. In his view, creativity has four dimensions: creativity as a product, creativity as a capacity, creativity as a process, and creativity as an aspect of the total person.[5] While creativity as a process is partially explained by Neihart and others as a form of regression to primitive mental process, the psychoanalytic definition of creative process does not explain fully the nonscientific dynamics of creativity mentioned above. In Tryk's view, creativity refers more to capacity and process and in particular how it relates to human suffering, including physical and mental disabilities or afflictions.

In presenting still a different definition of creativity, Charles Brenner commented about the value of creative work as viewed by others and stated that "creativity, like beauty, lies in the eyes and mind of the beholder, not in the psychodynamics of the individual who is called creative, however justified the appellation may be. It is the value judgment of one's fellow creatures that decides whether one is to be called creative or not. If one leaves that judgment to one side, everyone deserves to be called creative at every moment."[6] Therefore a person may be viewed as a celebrated artist today, but if the glamor of his art fades away, his work may be judged in the future as being merely banal.

The opposite change of opinion can also occur. For example, Vincent van Gogh was often disregarded as an artist during his lifetime because he lived in poverty, but Bouguereau, a contemporary painter of van Gogh, was well known and acclaimed as a master painter. Today, however, the genius of van Gogh is now widely appreciated, while Bouguereau is hardly known to most people.[7]

CREATIVITY AND HEALING

Defining creativity is difficult, and when we speak of creativity in the context of life crisis and healing, a clear definition becomes even more elusive. Neihart reviewed certain studies that suggest that "artistic endeavours heal the artist, whose work is then healing others."[8] However, many of these types of studies focus on a subgroup of the population of artists, especially writers, poets, and visual artists. Many artists use their work to save their mind and to express deep emotion. In the field of occupational and expressive therapies (such as art, music, poetry, or dance therapy), the act of painting, writing, or composing can not only serve as a form of catharsis but also as a valuable means of expression of self-knowledge. It may also enhance emotional stability and understanding of internal conflicts, which may lead to a possible solution.

Understanding creativity is as difficult as defining it, and when we speak of creativity in the context of life crises and adversities, its definition becomes even more complex. In view of the recent discovery that a relationship exists between creativity (in terms of high achievement in arts, music, writing . . .) and bipolar illness (manic depression), there may be neuropsychological pathways that connect these two phenomena. Richards and Kinney propose that the creativity observed in bipolar patients might serve as a "compensatory advantage" to the risk of this illness. To support this hypothesis, they cite the following medical finding: patients who suffer from sickle-cell anemia or who are carriers of it may become resistant to contracting malaria. This suggests the possibility that vulnerability to one illness may give the human body resistance to another.[9]

In pharmacology, it has been noted that certain side effects of one medication in treating a disease may serve as a remedy in the treatment of another ailment. Therefore such double-edged effects of pathology or treatment indicate that there may be more than one pathway in the development of an illness or its treatment. In supporting this argument that creativity can counter the effects of bipolar disorder, Flach suggests that "all creative arts entail disrupting an existing homeostatic structure and subsequently synthesizing a new, more adaptive one. This cycle is a necessary part of the healthy response to stressful events."[10]

In analyzing how creativity can assist those who are suffering emotionally, K. A. Breheny suggests that growth through suffering requires a shift of perspective in our minds. In other words, we must not think of ourselves as being alone in the universe and should instead consider ourselves, despite all the difficulties we encounter, to be connected to something infinite. When we make this shift, we take our suffering out of its dark isolation and view it in the larger context of life and the universe. We realize that there have been many more people, other than just ourselves, who have gone through the same suffering or worse. Such a realization can give new meaning to our existential crisis and put it in a new context, and this new meaning may be a turning point in our accepting a new reality about ourselves.

Although creativity can be a useful catalyst for healing, it can also be misused and can cause emotional and psychological damage. For example, in an effort to maximize creative productivity, some ambitious, creative individuals sometimes drive themselves to their maximum limit, neglecting their basic needs for sleep, proper nutrition, exercise, family, and social contact in a frenzy of creative activity day after day. This type of high-risk creative activity, however, often produces serious consequences. Many such individuals may experience isolation or depression and may attempt to self-medicate or resort to abusing alcohol or drugs. They may also face a wide range of problems resulting from their exclusive focus on their creative activity, such as marital conflicts and breakdown in family life.

Some creative people may believe that these behavioral changes are an integral part of the creative process. As a result, they may refuse therapeutic intervention, fearing that it may repress their creativity. Many of them may even attempt to justify a certain mental state by attempting to pattern their lives after famous writers such as Dostoyevsky and Hemingway, who both struggled with depression.[11]

KNOWLEDGE AND IMAGINATION IN CREATIVITY

Aristotle believed that the human brain possessed three internal senses: memory, reasoning, and imagination. Modern scientific thinking tends to emphasize knowledge, memory, and reasoning, but—strangely enough—it often overlooks the role of imagination in creativity. Yet there can be no question that imagination is crucial to any creative endeavor. Unlike reason, which often demands that a problem be solved in an orderly fashion, imagination often follows a disorderly path in reaching a creative goal. This does not mean, however, that imagination is inferior to reason. For example, 'Abdu'l-Bahá described imagination as being one of the attributes of the rational soul. According to Paul Claudel, "order is the pleasure of reason but disorder is the delight of the imagination."[12]

The word *imagination* stems from the word *image*, which also means *metaphor*. It is defined as the faculty of making mental images, but its definition is complex, and its extent can't be measured.

Imagination, however, does not necessarily equate with intelligence, and not every intelligent person is imaginative or creative. Creativity also does not appear to be weakened by sensory deprivation, as many people are very creative in spite of certain sensory impediments. For example, Beethoven was able to imagine combinations of musical sounds and create new musical compositions in spite of his deafness.[13]

Imagination may work on the conscious or subconscious level. During daydreams or fantasies, for example, we are aware of our imagination, but many of our creative solutions or developments may begin on a subconscious level without our conscious awareness. For example, if we are working intensely on solving a problem, we may find no solution in sight. Some time later, however, while relaxing or taking a walk, we may find the solution. This is because our imagination has been working on a subconscious level, assisted by stored knowledge, and its work has led to the solution. Does the spirit that possesses the qualities of knowledge and imagination play a role in this process? Is it possible that some of the early believers of the Bahá'í Faith discovered the truth and the Promised One through interaction of the soul and the faculty of knowledge and imagination? What is the role of spiritual inspiration in discovering the truth? When Thomas Edison was working on a new invention, for example, he would sometimes relax in an easy chair to await the solution. To avoid falling asleep, he would hold a heavy weight in each hand. If he fell into a sound sleep, his muscles would relax, and the weight would fall to the floor, waking him up so that he would not miss reaching a solution.[14]

MIND, BODY, AND SPIRIT

We are essentially spiritual beings grounded in a material world. Like seeds planted in the soil to grow, we need to break through the matrix of this material world and develop our potential. The purpose of this development is to serve and to be part of an everlasting civilization. Civilization itself is a creative process.

'Abdu'l-Bahá identified three degrees of reality in the world of humanity: the body, the soul, and the spirit. Humans and animals share the reality of physical existence in that they both possess the faculty of the senses. But unlike the animal, human beings possess a "rational soul, the human intelligence." 'Abdu'l-Bahá points out that human intelligence mediates between the body and spirit. This statement seems to relate the human intelligence, or rational soul, to the mind. He further elaborates that "when man does not open his mind and heart to the blessings of the spirit, he becomes inferior to the inhabitants of the lower animal kingdom . . . If, on the contrary, the spiritual nature of the soul has been so strengthened that it holds the material side in subjection, then does the man approach the Divine . . ."[15]

In another statement, 'Abdu'l-Bahá makes an analogy illustrating the intermediary role of the rational soul between the body and the spirit. He states that the tree is the intermediary between the seed and the fruit: "When a soul has in it the life of the spirit, then does it bring forth good fruit and become a divine tree."[16] Extending this analogy further, we can deduce that creativity is a product of the capacity of the mind and its fruit. If the soul be turned toward spiritual horizons, spiritual progress will result. If it is turned toward the material world, then the outcome will be material.

The mind, as described by 'Abdu'l-Bahá, is the power of the human spirit or the rational soul. He said, "Spirit is the lamp; mind is the light which shines from the lamp. Spirit is the tree, and the mind is the fruit. Mind is the perfection of the spirit, and its essential quality, as the sun's rays are the essential necessity of the sun."[17]

On the basis of this analogy, we can consider the mental faculties, such as intelligence, imagination, memory, reason, comprehension, and the power of discovery as being collectively referred to as the mind, the light within the lamp of the spirit. Thus the mind is endowed with high spiritual capacity, and consequently creativity—whether material or spiritual—emanates from that special source. The natural strength of these intellectual faculties will have important bearing on our perception of life and creativity.

The mental faculties of the mind that are closely related to the development of creativity are intelligence, imagination, and the power of discovery. Creativity can be either material or spiritual. Material aspects of creativity have given rise to the development of material civilization, scientific discoveries and inventions, artistic productivity, and other forms of progress. Spiritual creativity can include, for example, discovery of spiritual truth, unraveling the mysteries of life and the universe, championing the cause of social justice, the betterment of mankind, or care for the sick and suffering.

According to the Bahá'í writings, there is a close relationship between the mind and the human spirit, although in English, two different words—spirit and soul—are used. 'Abdu'l-Bahá indicates that the human spirit and the rational soul designate the same thing.[18]

As to the body, it is the physical frame through which the soul expresses its power. The body is mortal and is composed of material elements that are subject to composition and decomposition. The body is like a physical instrument for the soul to accomplish its potential in the journey of this life. The soul is nonphysical and free from decomposition; it is immortal. As Shoghi Effendi has written, "Physical ailments, no matter how severe, cannot bring any change in the inherent condition of the soul."[19]

Mental faculties are closely connected to the soul or human spirit. According to 'Abdu'l-Bahá, they are, in reality, "the inherent properties of the soul, even as the radiation of light is the essential property of the sun . . . The mind comprehendeth the abstract by the aid of the concrete, but the soul hath limitless manifestations of its own. The mind is circumscribed, the soul limitless. It is by the aid of such senses as those of sight, hearing, taste, smell and touch, that the mind comprehendeth, whereas the soul is free from all agencies."[20]

The above view of body and soul is very different from the reductionist concept of the French philosopher René Descartes, who in his classic *Treatise of Man* considered the body as a machine and denied the concept of the soul as a life force. He believed that the pineal gland at the base of the brain was the seat of the soul or consciousness.[21]

Descartes concluded that the unity of consciousness is made possible by the fact that the pineal gland is the sole part of the brain that is not double in structure—that is it does not exist in both hemispheres of the brain. This theory—the assigning of consciousness (or the soul) to an anatomical part of the body—was inconsistent, however, with Descartes' ideology about the separation of body and soul. Nevertheless, he persisted in his concept—known as Cartesian dualism—of the independence of mind from the body. In spite of its popularity, Descartes' view has been criticized by skeptics who refer to it as the "ghost in the machine" idea. [22] One might ask how the soul, which is a nonmaterial entity, could reside in a gland that is material. More intriguing is the question of what would happen if the pineal gland were to be surgically removed or split. Would consciousness disappear or be split?

Human beings are endowed with both spiritual and physical capacities that are interrelated. For example, human intelligence connects the human spirit and the body, creating a harmonious relationship that is critical for physical and spiritual progress.

LIMITS OF OUR KNOWLEDGE

The human being is a marvelous creation with much complexity. It contains biological, psychological, and spiritual dimensions, all of which make us human. Our knowledge of ourselves should therefore also embrace all these dimensions. Eric Cassell has written, "Persons cannot be reduced to their parts so that they can be better understood. Reductionistic scientific methods, so successful in other areas of human biology, do not help us to comprehend whole persons."[23]

Human curiosity is an asset in penetrating the world of the unknown and breaking the barriers of the mysteries of the universe. "Man is in the highest degree of materiality, and at the beginning of spirituality; that is to say, he is the end of imperfection and the beginning of perfection. He is at the last degree of darkness, and at the beginning of light."[24] Praiseworthy as curiosity and the creative attempt to uncover the mystery of life may be, there is a limit to the extent to which our mind can unravel the divine reality or essence. Bahá'u'lláh's* emphatic statement is a testimony to this limitation:

> O Salman! All that the sages and mystics have said or written have never exceeded, nor can they ever hope to exceed, the limitations to which man's finite mind hath been strictly subjected. To whatever heights the mind of the most exalted of men may soar, however great the depths which the detached and understanding heart can penetrate,

---

* The Prophet-Founder of the Bahá'í Faith.

such mind and heart can never transcend that which is the creature of their own conceptions and the product of their own thoughts. The meditations of the profoundest thinker, the devotions of the holiest of saints, the highest expressions of praise from either human pen or tongue, are but a reflection of that which hath been created within themselves, through the revelation of the Lord, their God. Whoever pondereth this truth in his heart will readily admit that there are certain limits which no human being can possibly transgress. Every attempt which, from the beginning that hath no beginning, hath been made to visualize and know God is limited by the exigencies of His own creation—a creation which He, through the operation of His own Will and for the purposes of none other but His own Self, hath called into being. Immeasurably exalted is He above the strivings of human mind to grasp His Essence, or of human tongue to describe His mystery.[25]

3

Resilience as a
Creative Response to Suffering

*"Character cannot be developed in ease and quiet. Only through experience
of trial and suffering can the soul be strengthened, ambition inspired, and
success achieved."*

—*Helen Keller*

The word *resilience* comes from the Latin *resilire,* meaning to "spring back,
to resume a prior position or form after being stretched or pressed."

Luthar et al. define resilience as a "process encompassing positive
adaptation within the context of significant adversity." Other studies cited
by Kim-Cohen et al. show that two factors are important in any definition of
resilience: exposure to risk and evidence of good adjustment. Diane Coutu
has identified three characteristics that resilient people possess: 1) a deep
belief that is often buttressed by strongly held values; 2) recognition that
life is meaningful; and 3) an innate ability to improvise. She believes that
these three characteristics apply to individuals as well as to organizations.
Furthermore, Coutu points out that although it is commonly believed that
resilience stems from an optimistic nature, such resilient optimism tends to
be realistic and not a "rose-colored thinking," which may lead to disaster.[1]

RESILIENCE AS A CREATIVE PROCESS

Making sense out of a life crisis and deriving meaning from it are two
major characteristics of resilience. However, a more important building
block of resilience in the face of adversity is having faith during troubled
times. Having the capacity to recognize meaning in hardship and being
determined to bounce back through faith and realism prevents one from
falling into a position of hopelessness. This capability to rise above human
limitations is a creative act of survival, and it is a bridge from adversity to
future fulfillment.[2]

Lepore and Revenson identify three distinct uses of the term *resilience* in literature concerning stress and trauma that reflect different dimensions of resilience. These consist of recovery, resistance, and reconfiguration (that is, reshaping individual thinking and behavior to adapt to trauma). Resilience has been conceptualized as a process that involves dynamic interactions between risk and protective factors in various stages of human life. The authors use the analogy of a tree blowing in the wind in order to explain these three facets of resilience. When a tree is blown by a strong wind, ordinarily it bends to accommodate the wind; otherwise it will break. After the wind stops, the tree resumes its original upright position. This reflects the fact that elasticity is a characteristic of resilience. Likewise, a stressor can disrupt the normal state of function of a person. But after the stress passes, the person resumes his or her normal state of functioning. This is an optimal level of adaptation.[3]

In the tree analogy, the reaction of the tree to the wind depends on the nature and composition of the tree. For example, a soft and flexible tree such as a willow will react differently to a strong wind than a hard and rigid tree such as an oak. In human beings, the degree of flexibility and strength is attributed to biological factors and personality traits. However, environmental factors such as social support and upbringing are also important in acquiring resilience in the face of adversity.[4]

Calhoun and Tedeschi propose the notion of posttraumatic growth (PTG) as a possible outcome of life crisis and suffering. By posttraumatic growth is meant that difficult life struggles may lead individuals to change in a positive direction. However, these authors acknowledge that PTG is not a universal experience and that only some people—usually those with at least a moderate degree of coping capability—can develop this ability. Traumatic experiences may relate to the process of creativity as well.[5]

CHAOS, RESILIENCE, AND CREATIVITY

We live in a world that is full of complexity due to the various manifestations of natural, technological, and social phenomena. Complexity is not bad—on the contrary, it challenges and stimulates our mind to come up with creative responses. Our mind is also highly complex and normally adjusts to the complexity of our environment. Our body is a dynamic system that has to adapt and make necessary changes according to circumstances. It is like a traveler who crosses different time zones and whose biological clock has to adjust to the changes of time.

It is believed that the larger the number of parts in a system, the more complex the system is likely to be. The human brain, as a system, is highly organized and complex, with millions of neurons and countless neuronal messengers that transmit information and reactions to internal and external stimuli. Generally speaking, "complex systems are dynamic and not in equilibrium, they are like a journey, not a destination, and they may pursue a moving target."[6]

One possible response to complexity is to be resilient, which may result in a creative outcome. A resilient response to chaos can create a new pattern, or it may lend meaning to chaos and confusion. Although chaos often has a negative connotation and may be seen as a destructive force, in science it has a different meaning that is worth exploring briefly. Indeed, if we can make sense of chaos, we may find a deeper understanding of its role in our life.

Chaos theory is, in effect, a way of studying complexity. Complexity can be explained along one of three paths: the spiritual, the philosophical, and the scientific. The scientific path of complexity in relation to chaos is that "chaos implies the existence of unpredictable or random aspects in dynamic matters." This is not necessarily something negative or undesirable. Sometimes it can be positive, and one may be able to create "order out of chaos." For example, an organization, although successful, may be too rigid and regimented, unable to be flexible and adjust to environmental changes. Consequently, it may deteriorate and break down. In contrast, there may be another organization that is quite disorganized but able to adjust to changing circumstances and, as a result, begin to improve and progress. Henry Adams has said, "Chaos often breeds life, when order breeds habit." Although equilibrium is always desirable, sometimes it needs to change. In today's world, according to Bahá'u'lláh, "The world's equilibrium hath been upset through the vibrating influence of this most great, this new World Order. Mankind's ordered life hath been revolutionized through the agency of this unique, this wondrous System—the like of which mortal eyes have never witnessed."[7]

There seems to be a relationship or similarity between the development of creativity during mood swings and chaos theory. Creative activity often disrupts the homeostasis of the daily rhythm of life. This disruption often requires a new adaptation. Thus what was initially perceived as a disruption or chaotic development turns out to be a creative process with its own characteristics.

Chaos theory originated from an attempt to discover order in systems that appeared to be "disordered." In other words, chaos theory is really about finding the "underlying order in apparently random data." Ian Stewart, one of the pioneers in the field of chaos theory, believes that "the flapping of a single butterfly's wing today produces a tiny change in the state of the atmosphere. Over a period of time, what the atmosphere actually does diverges from what it would have done. So, in a month's time, a tornado that would have devastated the Indonesian coast doesn't happen. Or maybe one that wasn't going to happen, does."[8]

Taking the example of an illness as chaos, a break in the routine daily activities may function in certain persons as a positive disintegration (chaos) that leads to a new stage of life and inspires new production of art. When a system resets itself away from its initial condition, it may move to a new state of existence. Illness may, therefore, act as a turning point. But, in order to develop creativity, some additional factors, including imagination, innate talent, and skills, must be present.[9]

EXPECTATION AND SURVIVAL

Focusing on the future during a time of hardship can sometimes make the difference between survival and death. Viktor Frankl, writing of his concentration camp experiences, recounted that

One day a prisoner told his fellows he had had a strange dream. He dreamed that a voice spoke to him and asked whether he wanted to know anything at all—it could foretell the future. He answered: "I should like to know when this Second World War will end for me." Whereupon the dream voice replied "On March 30, 1945." It was the beginning of March when the prisoner narrated this dream. At the time he was very hopeful and in good spirits. But as the thirtieth of March came closer and closer, it began to seem less and less probable that the "voice" would be right. In the last days before the prophesied deadline the man gave way more and more to discouragement. On March 29 he was taken to the infirmary with a high fever and in a state of delirium. On the crucial thirtieth of March—the day when the Second World War was to end "for him"—he lost consciousness. Next day he was dead of typhus.

This experience underlined the role of hope and its fulfillment in human psycho-biological defence mechanism and immune system to overcome a disease. In this case, the goal was not attained, his disappointment over the voice's "false" prophecy prevailed and consequently as result of breakdown in his bodily endurance and defences he succumbed to a dormant infection.[10]

Frankl realized that, in a concentration camp, the most effective way to maintain a positive attitude was to have a goal in the future to look forward to. He wrote that, during one conversation he had during his imprisonment, two fellow inmates revealed to him that both of them were haunted by the fear of not being able to expect anything in life. After Frankl turned their attention to the future, each of them began to consider a concrete goal and a task awaiting them in the outside world. For example, one of them had published a series of books on geography, but the series was still incomplete. The other had a daughter abroad who loved him devotedly. Both of these prisoners survived the hardship of the concentration camp ordeals, and Frankl has noted, "Human life can be fulfilled not only in creating and enjoying, but also in suffering!"[11] Their goals, for them, were irreplaceable and critical, and this gave them hope and lent a meaning to their life in spite of all their suffering.

HAPPINESS AMIDST ADVERSITY

There is a prevailing impression that happiness amidst ordeals is a non-existent, if not strange, experience. Happiness is understood by many to be intimately connected to times of comfort, success, and prosperity. Yet there are stories of many individuals who are happy and contented in spite of suffering. This may be difficult to explain on the basis of materialistic psychology, as cause and effect do not follow a "logical" sequence. How often do we see a person who is blind, sorely afflicted by poverty and disease, who, due to inner strength or belief, radiates a sense of happiness and confidence? There must be a spiritual meaning in the experience that defies psychological defenses. Happiness in these individuals is not a symptom of a masochistic behavior nor of a break with reality, as in psychosis. It is an expression of contentment and acceptance of an unavoidable ordeal and submission to the will of God. As 'Abdu'l-Bahá has written, "Anyone can be happy in the state of comfort, ease, health, success, pleasure and joy; but if one will be happy and contented in the time of trouble, hardship and prevailing disease, it is the proof of nobility."[12]

In a materialistic society, however, happiness is often bound to material interest, wealth, or recognition. As success or failure is often associated with happiness or its loss, it is necessary to thoroughly define and elaborate on the concept of happiness.

There is a difference between pleasure and happiness. Pleasure is an experience of physical satisfaction in response to personal or environmental stimuli that activate the pleasure center of the brain. It can be induced artificially by stimulant drugs. True happiness is a spontaneous and lasting experience of a spiritual nature. Erich Fromm makes a distinction between joy and pleasure. He defines pleasure as the satisfaction of desire and believes that we live in a world of "joyless pleasure." In his view, the pleasures of contemporary society lead to different degrees of excitement. But this excitement is not conducive to joy. "In fact the lack of joy makes it necessary to seek ever new, ever more exciting pleasures." True happiness is a state of the soul, not the body, although the body is the frame through which happiness is outwardly expressed. But inwardly, true happiness is a spiritual experience. 'Abdu'l-Bahá describes two kinds of happiness—spiritual and material: "As to material happiness, it never exists; nay it is but imagination, an image reflected in mirrors, a specter and shadow. Consider the nature of material happiness. It is something which but slightly removes one's afflictions; yet the people imagine it to be joy, delight, exultation and blessing. All the material blessings, including food, drink, etc., tend only to allay thirst, hunger and fatigue. They bestow no delight on the mind nor pleasure on the soul; nay, they furnish only the bodily wants. So this kind of happiness has no real existence."[13]

To elaborate on the spiritual aspects of joy and suffering, it is necessary to state that knowledge is of two kinds: one kind is objective and based on perceived knowledge, while the other is subjective and intuitive. The former is associated with the work of the mind, while the latter is the expression of inherent qualities of the soul. Material knowledge is acquired through learning and individual effort, while spiritual knowledge is an innate experience. To examine the spiritual and material nature of joy and happiness, we need to resort to spiritual and scientific means to come to a clear understanding of the phenomenon. The task, however, may be complex. A great spiritual educator once asked a scientist if science could distinguish a teardrop from a drop of water. The answer was "yes," given the chemical composition of these two drops. Then the educator asked if the scientist could recognize with certainty whether the teardrop was one of joy or of sorrow without knowing its source. The answer was "no." This answer showed the limit of science in elucidating the source of a teardrop. Science can unravel the details of tangible, observable, and measurable objects, but it is unable to draw a meaning and feeling about it. 'Abdu'l-Bahá also states, "The happiness and greatness, the rank and station, the pleasure and peace, of an individual have never consisted in his personal wealth, but rather in his excellent character, his high resolve, the breadth of his learning, and his ability to solve difficult problems."[14]

4

Dimensions of Resilience and Environmental Factors

"O Son of Man! My calamity is My providence, outwardly it is fire and vengeance, but inwardly it is light and mercy."

—*Bahá'u'lláh*

Human ability to respond to disturbing life events and suffering largely depends on internal as well as external resources and capabilities. Although responses vary from person to person, the experience of life crises can have enabling effects for all people. For example, Kathleen McGowan writes, "Hurricanes, house fires, cancer, white-water rafting accidents, plane crashes, vicious attacks in dark alleyways. Nobody asks for any of it. But to their surprise, many people find that enduring such a harrowing ordeal ultimately changes them for the better. Their refrain might go something like this: 'I wish it hadn't happened, but I'm a better person for it.'"[1]

Studies on children show that only rarely are children emotionally disabled by the force of ordeals, even with the most severe stressors and under the most glaring adversities. Likewise, most adults who suffer personal losses or crises do not become clinically depressed as a result of disturbing life events. This observation suggests that a person's response to social and environmental conditions is partly due to his or her genetic influences. Therefore the genetic makeup of a person is a factor in how a person affects or is affected by his or her environment, and as a result, an individual is sometimes able to select and shape his or her own environment based on the genes he or she has inherited. Thus the individual's disturbing experiences and reactions to them are due to nature as well as nurture.[2]

Resistance to life stress and crisis, however, is not absolute. It depends on environmental and constitutional conditions, and the extent of resistance is not fixed.[3] Let's suppose, for example, that two persons working in a company with similar jobs and family situations suddenly lose their jobs.

31

Naturally, their initial reactions are likely to be a feeling of sadness due to the financial impact of this loss on the family. One may develop clinical depression, while the other does not, and it may be discovered later that the depressed person had a personal or family history of this illness and thus was genetically predisposed to such a reaction, while the other was free from this susceptibility.

A different scenario would be if neither of these two had any personal or family history of depression. But searching for a solution to the loss of a job in a difficult time may lead one person to panic or to have a depressive reaction while another person manages to avoid such a reaction. It may turn out that the one who had the breakdown lacked social skills, problem-solving ability, and support. As a result, the individual with the breakdown is more vulnerable to life crises. Social support often has a buffering effect with a protective function in the face of stressors.

RESILIENCE OF CHILD SURVIVORS OF CONCENTRATION CAMPS

Research has shown that exposure to prolonged and excessive trauma will have long-term adverse effects on physical and psychological aspects of health as well as on the longevity of survivors. Many survivors, for example, suffer symptoms of anxiety, depression, fear, social withdrawal, and somatic symptoms of emotional distress. Although there have been extensive reports on the negative psychological and physical consequences in the lives of trauma survivors who suffered from Nazi persecution while they were young adults or older, reports on survivors who were children when that tragedy occurred are scarce. In one such study, John J. Segal and Morton Weinfeld from McGill University compared young adults— ages nineteen through thirty-six who were native-born citizens of Canada and the United States—with children of Jews who had survived the Holocaust and immigrated to these countries after World War II. The researchers sought to examine whether the child survivors of the Holocaust were indeed faring better than adult survivors, so they followed these two groups for forty years.[4]

They found that those survivors who were teenagers or adults at the end of World War II showed long-term effects of prolonged stress. However, those survivors who were children or preteens at the end of World War II (the children were 2–9 years old, the preteens were 10–13 years old, the teenagers were 14–18 years old, and the adults were 19–24 years old) did not show the same level of stress as their older counterparts. They were followed for forty years and tested in the 1980s.[5]

This study raises the following question: what protected the children and preteens of World War II from the symptoms of psychological trauma, compared with the teenagers and adults of World War II? The authors suggest that the following factors were sources of resilience and possible protection: disposition, social support, coping or defense style, and cognitive development. These factors have been reported in literature to play a role in mitigating the adverse consequences of psychological trauma.[6]

The author explored another study of a group of adults in 1985 who, at the end of World War II, had been children aged three to eight years old and had for the most part been in concentration camps. All had lost their parents during the war and had grown up in orphanages with a caring staff. This group was compared to a second group of those who, at the end of the war, had been ages eight through eighteen years old while in Nazi extermination camps and had also been placed in orphanages with caring staff members. It was noted that, despite the lengthy time these individuals had lived in adverse circumstances, both groups were functioning well in their social, vocational, and family lives forty years later.

Why did these two groups do well in spite of childhood suffering? What they had in common was the presence of one or more persons who continued caring for them over many years despite being initially subjected to alienating behavior. This caring environment most likely helped them to cope with the traumatic experiences of the concentration camps.

Other factors that helped the survivors of childhood adversity were coping skills and defense mechanisms. One of the defense mechanisms was repression of negative childhood experiences, and this repression facilitated the long-term adaptation of the child survivors.[7] These defense mechanisms probably worked better in the younger age group because the older group was exposed to a more severe form of trauma. Another contributing factor was that, in general, adults have more ability to cognitively process any threat and evaluate their vulnerability.

Therefore, they are more likely to report stress-related anxiety. Children's cognitive ability for that process is limited. They may show over-reaction immediately after disaster, but then it is mitigated.

Usually, during the adolescent period perception of vulnerability and appraisal of threat become more developed. However, these findings—including the role of repression, perception of a threat, and response to it—require more in-depth research, exploration, and confirmation.

Three major sources of resilience are postulated in the literature as follows:

1. A consistent, caring, and supportive environment or network
2. Innate disposition (easy temperament and active coping)
3. Experiences that would augment self-esteem, efficacy, and cognitive development.[8]

ATTITUDE, RESILIENCE, AND COPING

Human attitude and a sense of identity are interrelated. Attitudes are difficult to change because they are a combination of cognitive, emotional, and behavioral habits. As a result, when a person's behavioral attitudes are developed, he often becomes resistant to change, and any attempts to break through this resistance can evoke feelings of resentment, fear, and anxiety. This is because attitude has become so much part of the person's self identity that such attempts are perceived as a threat to one's integrity. Change of habits, therefore, requires a change of thinking and motivation as well as the will to change. This is why, as noted above, children are more easily able to adapt to stressful situations, as their sense of self identity is still unformed, while adults already have a well-developed sense of identity.

Resilience, therefore, is related to behavioral attitudes and identity, and their expression through perseverance is based on one's identity. For example, hope, a positive attitude, and a realistic optimism are qualities that reinforce resilience. Other coping skills are a high level of autonomy, problem-solving and decision-making capability, the capacity to set one's own personal goals and priorities, the ability to consult, and the avoidance of blind imitation. Curiosity, an openness to criticism, plus flexibility combined with determination are also essential qualities to coping with stressful situations. Optimistic and hopeful people, therefore, have greater chances of bouncing back from adversity and improving their situation. "Hope helps a person endure through difficult times and realistic optimism provides thoughts and images of things turning out well. Coping is an interactive process, different for each individual, in which a person keeps learning how to be better at handling difficult physical, mental and emotional challenges. Resilient people can combine them all."[9]

FACING LIFE STRESS

Psychological stress is one of the most pervasive phenomena of our time, and it can affect people from all walks of life. It is a condition that occurs when there is a discrepancy between the demands made upon a person and his capability to respond to those demands.[10] Coping with psychological stress is a process that largely depends upon human ability to appraise intelligently the environmental demands and to respond to them successfully. Two-thirds of office visits to family physicians in North America are prompted by stress-related problems. For example, burnout is a phenomenon that occurs as a result of prolonged exposure to work-related stress, and some of its symptoms are emotional exhaustion and personal devaluation. Psychological stress can originate from within the person, as in the case of internal conflicts and prejudices, or it can be caused by external events such as natural or manmade disasters, social injustice, inflation, unemployment, social deprivation, or racism. Different people respond differently to the same stress.

Linford Rees reported a patient whose main complaint was an intense anxiety. As the psychiatrist began to ask a series of questions about the patient's medical history, the patient commented that he could tell the doctor exactly what was the matter with him. The therapist asked him to please do so. The patient replied that the problem was his work: he was employed in a fruiterer's shop and his job was to separate the large oranges from the small ones. The therapist encouraged him to explain further. But the patient replied, "That's it. It's decisions, decisions, decisions!"[11]

As this example shows, an individual's perception and interpretation of a conflict and his attitude toward it have an important bearing on the quality and extent of that person's reaction to that threat. If the person can make sense out of a crisis and draw some objective conclusion from it that would give new meaning to his life, the stressful event will more likely be perceived as less threatening.

In societies where there is excessive emphasis on material success as the main source of happiness, people may become more vulnerable to stress. Such an attachment makes their separation from material excess more difficult. With modern scientific discoveries, man experiences an illusory sense of omnipotence and power to control his environment and conquer the universe. The popular tales of Superman and his power are a symbolic expression of many ideas that our present generation entertains. In such a climate, failure to master control over life circumstances becomes a new source of anxiety.

BIOLOGICAL AND PSYCHOLOGICAL RESPONSES TO LIFE STRESS

The human brain produces both its own anxiety-inducing and anxiety-reducing substances, and the latter are of special importance in coping with stress and suffering. For example, the release of endorphins by the brain is one way in which the body responds to psychological and physical stressors (stress-producing factors). Endorphins (morphine-like substances) are natural neurotransmitters that not only alleviate pain, but also promote pleasure and manage stress responses. Over a dozen kinds of endorphins have been identified. Endorphin receptors are found in the brain and other parts of the body. The surge of endorphin production represents the body's response to physical and emotional pain and suffering.[12]

Among medical procedures, acupuncture is known to have the ability to trigger the release of pituitary endorphins that can affect the perception and experience of pain. Migraine patients are reported to suffer from a deficiency of beta endorphin as compared to a control group.[13] There are indications that the practices of biofeedback, acupuncture, and meditation enhance the release of these substances. For more details about endorphins, please see chapter 8.

Our perception of stressors will play an important role in the way we react to life events. When a stressor is perceived as being meaningless, it may appear more disquieting. Although making sense of a trauma and having insight into its nature may help our coping process, it may not completely alleviate the tension and agony of a trauma. Therefore, besides psychological defenses, we need reliance on a higher power for our existential crises.

Hans Selye, a renowned physician who did extensive research about stress, stated that although stressors may be qualitatively different, they may elicit the same biological responses: "Stress is the nonspecific response of the body to any demand made upon it . . . it is immaterial whether the agent or situation we face is pleasant or unpleasant; all that counts is the intensity of the demand for readjustment or adaptation. The mother who is suddenly told that her only son died in battle suffers a terrible mental shock; if years later it turns out that the news was false and the son unexpectedly walks into her room alive and well, she experiences extreme joy. The specific results of the two events, sorrow and joy, are completely different—in fact, opposite to each other—yet their stressor effect—the nonspecific demand to readjust herself to an entirely new situation—may be the same."[14] In brief, psychological reactions to two different events may cause an identical biological outcome.

Selye identified two kinds of stress: eustress and distress. Eustress is the positive and essentially valuable form of stress that will contribute to the well-being of an organism. When stress becomes unpleasant or harmful, it will result in discomfort and distress.[15]

There are two dimensions in traumatic experiences and other distressful events: objective and subjective. Most objective traumas are external and observable such as bodily injury, physical violence, rape, or disease. The subjective aspect involves human perception and interpretation of the objective trauma. The subjective assessment of a traumatic event can exaggerate or minimize the impact of the trauma. Some individuals may not remember that traumatic experiences have occurred, while others may assume that a trauma has taken place without having evidence for its occurrence. The intensity of response to trauma may be similar to the dose response in medicine. It is also similar to the consumption of alcohol. When a person consumes alcohol, the heavier the alcohol intake, the higher the likelihood of intoxication. Similarly, the more severe the trauma, the more harmful the effect. But human response to life crisis such as trauma does not always follow dose response principles. Other factors are involved that may influence the intensity of the perception of the trauma such as personality traits, sociocultural elements, and genetic predisposition. This may explain why different individuals facing the same traumatic experience may differ in their responses.[16]

The interaction of personality traits and environment can determine our reaction to stressors. For example, it is well known that some medical students in the course of their clinical studies of various diseases may worry that they too may have the disease that they have been reading about while others may not.

Traumatic experiences may be of two types: man-made traumas such as physical or psychological abuse, combat, or rape, and natural trauma and disasters. The man-made traumatic experiences can be far more difficult to bear than those experienced as a result of natural disasters such as hurricanes, tsunamis, or volcanic eruptions.[17] One likely interpretation of this difference is that large-scale natural disasters are beyond human control, often strike with a single blow, and mobilize people to help one another to survive. The man-made assaults and injuries, however, are intended by human beings to cause serious harm, may go on for a long time, and can often be avoided.

SPIRITUAL ASPECTS OF COPING
A spiritual perspective can often result in a deeper understanding of life crises.[18] It can be a great source of hope and strength.

Prayer helps us to accept life's challenges and is an important part of spiritual coping. Throughout history, prayer has been one of the most common means of asking for divine assistance in facing life crisis and adversity. Prayers are also believed to be beneficial for both spiritual and material healing. If healing is in the best interest of the patient, it will be granted. But prayer depends on the will of God. Research shows that prayer and supplication for assistance have a healing effect in patients; however, the mechanism of the effect is not known, nor is it to be assumed that medical treatment should be abandoned because of reliance on prayer.[19]

The goal of the human soul is to achieve greater perfection. This process of striving for perfection, or spiritual development, is independent of physical growth and development. Similarly, the experience of joy and sorrow of the soul is independent of that of the physical body.[20]

'Abdu'l-Bahá describes the wisdom of the appearance of the spirit in the body as follows: "The human spirit is a Divine Trust, and it must traverse all conditions, for its passage and movement through the conditions of existence will be the means of its acquiring perfections. Such perfection is attained by individual effort and through the power of the Holy Spirit. "The confirmations of the Spirit are all those powers and gifts which some are born with and which men sometimes call genius, but for which others have to strive with infinite pains. They come to that man or woman who accepts his life with radiant acquiescence."[21]

Some of the spiritual responses to life stress and crises are greater reliance on personal faith and belief, higher capacity to accept pain and suffering, awareness of one's own helplessness and imperfection, acknowledgment of a supreme source of might and perfection (the Creator), reliance on prayer and meditation, and an increased sense of purpose in life. The spiritual power and strength to overcome adversities stem from one's own faith and conviction in the Divine Manifestation. In the words of 'Abdu'l-Bahá: "As you have faith, so shall your powers and blessings be."[22]

The following story illustrates how grief over the death of a loved one was changed into comfort. One day 'Abdu'l-Bahá was asked by a lady to visit her sick child in 'Akká. He came, bringing two pink roses, which He gave to the little one. Then, turning to the lady, He said with a voice full of love, "You must be patient!" That evening the child passed away. When the mother asked 'Abdu'l-Bahá the reason, he said, "There is a garden of God. Human beings are trees growing in that garden. Our Heavenly Father is the Gardener. When the Gardener sees a little tree in a place which is too small for its development, He prepares a suitable and more beautiful place where it may grow and bear fruit. Then He transplants that little tree. The other trees are surprised and say, 'This was a lovely tree. Why did the Gardener uproot it?' Only the Divine Gardener knows the reason. You are weeping, but if you could see the beauty of the place where your child is, you would no longer be sad. She is now free, like a bird, and she is chanting divine, happy melodies. If you could see that sacred Garden yourself, you would not be content to remain here on earth. Yet, this is where your duty now lies."[23]

RESILIENCE IN TIME OF HARDSHIP

Helen Keller once wrote, "Character cannot be developed in ease and quiet. Only through experience of trial and suffering can the soul be strengthened, ambition inspired and success achieved."[24] Different people respond differently to life crisis and hardship. Some feel weak and helpless, while others feel enraged and lash out at those around them. Still others rely on their personal insight and experience, and they move forward with confidence. Some blame the world and how unfair it is, while others search to discover a solution to the crisis they are facing.

Resilience is a state of mind in the face of life challenges. Overall, our resilience is formed by a combination of our genetic makeup and psychosocial factors including coping strategies and attitudes that help us to bounce back and overcome hardship in a healthy and creative way. Resilient people are confident, energetic, optimistic, perceptive, and self-reliant. They are able to rely on divine assistance, are systematic in their approach to solving problems, and avoid assuming the position of being a victim. They can see beyond the gloom of the immediate future and have hope for change. "This, too, shall pass" is the insightful impression of resilient people. They are survivors!

Resilient individuals do not deny the reality of pain and grief in the face of life challenges, but they are determined to overcome this reality with perseverance and positive thinking.

A spiritual perception of life can be a great source of hope and strength. The persecution sustained by the early believers in each of the world's religions is a testimony of unusual and heroic resilience. Here, reliance on divine power dissipated any trace of doubt or fear of destruction.

Although resilience is a reflection of one's state of mind, it also relies on one's physical and psychological resources and strength. A body weakened by chronic illness, exhaustion, isolation, addiction, and poor sleeping and eating habits may have little resilience, although willpower can sometimes prevail over a frail bodily condition.

Many people have had to face and survive tragedy or disease in spite of seemingly insurmountable challenges. The following is an example from the athletic world.

LANCE ARMSTRONG: A CANCER SURVIVOR AND ATHLETE
Lance Armstrong stunned the world when he rode into the crowd-lined Champs Élysées in Paris on July 25, 2004, winning a record of six Tours de France and becoming one of the greatest athletes of all time in cycling races. For six consecutive years he had won the crown of the race in the heart of Europe, a heroic and matchless performance in the 101-year history of

the Tour de France. Eight years earlier, his physician had given him less than a 50 percent chance of recovery from the testicular cancer that had spread to his lungs and brain. Armstrong refused to accept his condition, however, and he fought the cancer head-on. His vigorous training and cycling, along with his unquenchable hope and determination to conquer his illness, brought him astonishing victories. In the end, Armstrong beat the odds, and he overcame the cancer.[25]

ACQUIRING RESILIENCE

Dr. Al Siebert believes that attitude and beliefs play a key role in individual resiliency, and he argues that self-motivated persons thrive in conditions of constant change. Siebert identifies several principles that influence people's resilience in the face of challenges and adversities.[26]

In our struggle with adversity, our minds and our habits will either create barriers or build bridges to a better future. An example of one kind of habit is our perception of "failure." In a society characterized by excessive competition and success-oriented lifestyle, "failure" is not acceptable. Consequently, people frequently are in a state of anxiety and fear of failure. Such fear and discontentment have a corrosive effect on resilient behavior. However, seeing failure as a springboard to future success creates a bridge rather than a barrier.[27]

Some people have a tendency to magnify and exaggerate the importance of an event: they tend to catastrophize the extent of a problem. Neither maximizing nor minimizing the impact of an event can objectively contribute to a solution. The extreme indulgence in negative thinking can be likened to a drop of ink that discolors an entire beaker of water.[28]

Life can be unfair, but this is good for personal growth. Resilient people find a way to overcome adversity and bounce back from setbacks, and this ability makes them stronger. Self-knowledge enhances individual resiliency, which is based on self-observation, freedom to experiment, and being receptive to ideas and feedback.[29] Patience and tenacity are other qualities that can help to overcome challenges. In a fast-food consumer society, patience is a rare commodity, but without patience and perseverance, many opportunities will be lost.

Building resiliency also requires the ability to acquire and improve our problem-solving and decision-making skills, to learn from errors, to maintain a sense of self-confidence, to think positively, to be optimistic, and to have a sense of humor. Reflection and meditation on life events and reliance on prayer for divine assistance will enhance a person's consciousness of meaning and purpose of life. Prayer by itself cannot replace reasoning, but neither can problem-solving or reasoning inspire hope without prayer and faith. On a collective level, consultation—a process of sharing thoughts and viewpoints—is a realistic approach to decision making. It is not blindly seeking the approval of others but rather evaluating facts to reach truth in the spirit of fellowship.

COPING SKILLS FOR LIFE CRISES

Coping skills and knowledge of personal resources are some of the qualities we need to acquire in the face of life crises. Dr. Steven Southwick from Yale University suggests some of the following factors, which are critical in dealing with life crisis.[30]

- Having a moral compass
  There are always difficult choices to make in traumatic circumstances of life. People often feel guilty because they haven't done well enough. But resilient individuals are confident that they took the right course of action in difficult situations.
- Meditation and reflection
  Meditation is powerful and helps us to cope with a crisis. With reflection, we reevaluate our life and discover new priorities.
- Acceptance
  Acceptance is a survival mechanism. When people accept the implication and meaning of a crisis, they can reflect to see if they have the power to change it. One prayer reads, "God grant me the serenity to accept the things I cannot change, the courage to change the things I can, and the wisdom to know the difference."[31]
- Social support and empathy
  Friends and relatives can help a person deal with the consequences of trauma.
- Exercise
  Exercise can enhance physical as well as mental resilience in the face of challenges. In laboratory rats, exercise stimulates nerve

growth in the hippocampus area of the brain. Research studies show that exercise can increase the production of endorphin in the brain. "Runner's high" may be related to the production of endorphins; however, this requires further exploration.

- Coping skills
  There are many skills one can acquire to deal with adversity.

Our perception of life crises can affect our approach to them. Once a couple announced to their parents that they wanted to move from New Jersey to New Zealand. The husband's mother was shocked and devastated by this decision, and she died a few months later. But the wife's mother reacted differently and said, "Oh, that's interesting. I look forward to visiting you there!" She visited them later at age eighty.[32]

PEACE AND SURRENDER IN A CANCER PATIENT

Dr. Jerri Nielsen was a forty-six-year-old physician working at the American research station at the South Pole. She loved the simplicity of life in this very remote part of the world. A few months into the pitch-dark winter of the South Pole, she discovered that she had breast cancer. Realizing that she was trapped there for the winter because no plane could land on the ice due to the extreme temperatures, Dr. Nielsen thought she might die before spring. Eventually she was evacuated and returned to the United States, where she underwent a mastectomy. Unfortunately, the surgery did not completely remove the cancer from her body, and after some time she learned that the cancer had spread to her bones. In an interview at this point in the progression of her illness she stated, "My experience at the pole had to do with accepting things that most people fear most deeply . . . It certainly had far more to do with peace and surrender than it did with courage. Being 'on the ice' was a great good fortune: It created a much greater clarity for me about what was essential in life. I'm not afraid of death. I've come to accept it as being part of life." After her realization that the cancer had metastasized to her bones, for three weeks she experienced a kind of terror. Then she felt "the most incredible peace" come over her.[33]

RESILIENCE AND CREATIVITY: PSYCHOSOCIAL AND SPIRITUAL PERSPECTIVES

Resilience is a virtue that is associated with courage, hope, and positive thinking. Courage, as opposed to fear, is an expression of conviction and faith. Early believers as well as heroes and heroines of various religions were empowered by religious teachings that strengthened their resolve and faith. The result was courage and a higher capacity to endure pain and suffering in upholding the standard of their beliefs. By contrast, those who were overcome with fear and became perplexed and ambivalent in the face of torment and persecution betrayed their mission.

There are countless examples in religious history of courage or fear. Judas, who was a devoted disciple of Christ, betrayed his Lord on the eve of Christ's crucifixion. A contrasting development occurred when, on the night before the execution of the Báb, the Prophet of the Bábí Religion, a young follower titled Anís (Mírzá Muḥammad-'Alíy-i-Zunúzí) offered his absolute obedience and thus fulfilled his wish to become the companion of the Báb, his Lord, at the time of His execution in Iran.

Creativity stems from knowledge and imagination, which stimulate a new perspective or reality expressed in art, science, religion, and other fields of human endeavor. Many innovators had a rich sense of imagination and foresight combined with a capacity to persevere until the task was accomplished. From Galileo and Newton to Einstein, there have been a range of discoveries in the sciences and arts. Likewise, in the history of religion, creative perceptions were inspired and stimulated through the divine teachings. Knowledge and faith, together with imagination, nurtured a high determination to overcome adversity and opposition and to break new ground for survival and triumph over oppression.

Resilience, hope, and positive thinking are not inborn; rather, they are acquired through life experience.[34] Optimism is another marker of resilience and creativity. However, one needs to be realistic in one's optimism. An unrealistic optimism may lead to negative consequences. A sense of helplessness and pessimism are also acquired, but whatever is acquired can also be transformed.

TURNING CRISIS INTO OPPORTUNITY:
"TURNING LEMONS INTO LEMONADE"

Research shows that experiencing hardship not only reinforces the development of resiliency but also enhances our ability to thrive under stress. Hardship can improve performance and stamina and, to some extent, mental health. Dr. Salvator R. Maddi and his associates at the University of Chicago have explored the question of why some people suffer from psychological or physical breakdowns when faced with a high level of distress while others seem to thrive.[35] In 1981 Illinois Bell Telephone (IBT) downsized from 26,000 employees to just over half that number within one year. Dr. Maddi and his research team had been following the IBT situation three years prior to the downsizing, and they evaluated the employees and then reported the results of their evaluations.

About two-thirds of the employees in the study suffered significant performance, leadership, and health declines because of the severe stress due to deregulation and disruptions related to their jobs. These negative effects included heart attacks, strokes, obesity, depression, substance abuse, and poor performance. Surprisingly, the remaining third of employees actually thrived during the crisis despite facing the same level of stressful experiences as their fellow workers. They were able to maintain their performance, health, and happiness, and they felt renewed enthusiasm.

In exploring what made the two groups so different, Dr. Maddi found that those who thrived maintained three key beliefs which enabled them to turn adversity into creative advantage: commitment, control, and positive attitudes. These three attitudes helped these employees to strive to be involved in the ongoing events (thus avoiding isolation), to try to influence outcomes (instead of lapsing into passivity and powerlessness), and to consider stressful changes, whether positive or negative, as opportunities for new learning.[36]

RESILIENCE AND HUMOR: NORMAN COUSINS

In his book *Anatomy of an Illness,* Norman Cousins insists that the mental attitudes of patients play an important role in the course of their disease.[37] The body's defenses against an illness depend to a large extent on the mechanisms of the hormonal and immune systems. These mechanisms themselves may be influenced in either a positive or negative way by a person's mental state. For example, one of the specific pathways between a person's emotional state and physiological activities is through the brain and pituitary gland, which releases hormones called endorphins. Cousins's personal experience with a serious and crippling disease illustrates the possible role of endorphins in pain reduction.

In 1964 Cousins suffered a very serious collagen disease, an arthritic disease of the connective tissue throughout his body. The resulting pain and inflammation severely affected the movement of his limbs.[38] As a medical journalist for the *Saturday Review*, he was highly knowledgeable about his condition, which he knew was serious. He was hospitalized and treated with heavy doses of aspirin, the long-term effects of which adversely affected his adrenal glands. His will to live, however, sustained him to fight the disease with tenacity and courage.

In the midst of his medical crisis, with no remission in sight, he came to the realization that a full exercise of affirmative emotions might have an enhancing effect on his body chemistry. He decided that laughter could be a factor in influencing positive recovery. While still in the hospital, with the help of others, he obtained copies of the spoofing television program *Candid Camera* and numerous comic films including some of the old "Marx Brothers" films. He then found a film projector, prepared the room, pulled down the blinds, and prepared the machine for a systematic program of laughter therapy. Years later, he wrote, "It worked. I made the joyous discovery that ten minutes of joyous belly laughter had an anesthetic effect and would give me at least 2 hours of pain-free sleep. When the pain-killing effect of the laughter wore off, we would switch on the motion picture projector again and not infrequently, it would lead to another 2 hours of pain-sleep interval. Sometimes the nurse read to me out of a trove of humour books."[39]

During this time, Cousins reflected on various questions such as how scientific was it to believe that laughter, as well as positive emotions in general, were affecting the body chemistry for a recovery? Lab tests before and several hours after laughter episodes showed a possible mitigation of his arthritic disorder. Increasingly large doses of vitamin C were added to his laughter treatment to help his immune system. This combination of laughter and vitamin C helped, and at the end of eight days he was able to move his thumbs without pain. After several months, he was able to move his arms, and he gradually regained the strength needed for other movements. Finally, he recovered sufficiently to resume his full-time job at the *Saturday Review*. Complete recovery came slowly, and year by year his mobility improved.

Cousins never accepted his specialists' verdict at the onset of his illness that his disease was progressive and incurable. His will to live, his resorting to positive emotions, and his holistic approach, along with the help of his physician, enabled him to overcome an otherwise serious and debilitating disease. This is also a story of creative vision of hope and struggle to succeed, and it reflects a partnership between a physician and a patient in beating back the odds.[40]

CHILDREN AND RESILIENCE

Learning resilience begins at home as early as infancy. Research in hardiness and resilience has been used by the American Psychological Association (APA) to help children, adolescents, and adults to better adapt to adversity, trauma, tragedy, threats, and other life crises. In the fall of 2003, the APA launched a school-based campaign called "Resilience for Kids & Teens" that taught the principles of resilience for problems in school or at home. The campaign included distribution of educational materials to two million fourth- through sixth-grade students and their teachers in the United States to help children learn the skills of resilience using "kid-friendly" language. The APA developed a partnership with the Discovery Health Channel for a national multimedia campaign that was designed to help Americans to cope and work through personal tragedy by learning strategies for resilience. This partnership went into effect in the wake of the September 11, 2001, tragedy.[41]

ACCUSTOMING CHILDREN TO HARDSHIP

Accustoming children to hardship increases their endurance and ability to cope in the face of adversity and distress. 'Abdu'l-Bahá, speaking of the education of children, states, "Bring them up to work and strive, and accustom them to hardship." He further says, "Hardship is any experience that requires strength and toughness of character to endure. Enduring hardship calls for the strength of will. Hardship is any task or situation for which there is no easy way out." But hardship does not imply that children should be subject to harsh, negative, and onerous experiences. Rather, they should be accustomed to hardship in a gradual and wise manner. 'Abdu'l-Bahá further notes, "In a time to come, morals will degenerate to an extreme degree. It is essential that children be reared in the Bahá'í way, that they may find happiness both in this world and the next. If not, they shall be beset by sorrows and troubles, for human happiness is founded upon spiritual behavior."[42]

Is there any relationship between hardship and the meaning of life? One possibility is that hardship links children to the purpose of life. The purpose of life is to develop spiritual qualities, such as virtues, as well as a noble character, and children who are accustomed to hardship are more able to withstand the tests and trials of life. Through hardship they develop self-discipline and become more confident, objective, and systematic in life. They realize that they should take responsibility for their actions and are able to find opportunity in crisis. The Universal House of Justice,* in supporting this concept, has written, "Love demands discipline, the courage to accustom them (children) to hardship, not to indulge their whims or leave them entirely to their own devices."[43]

VULNERABILITY AND RESILIENCE

Kim-Cohen et al. noted three factors that help to predict resilience adjustment in children. These are a child's characteristics, the parent-child relationship (cognitive stimulation, emotional warmth), and social support. The authors also identified two child-specific protective factors—a child's outgoing temperament and parental warmth toward the child. For example, children who possess an outgoing temperament and who demonstrate confidence and eagerness in their interactions with others, including unfamiliar adults, are perceived to have strengths and competencies.[44]

In their study of 1,116 pairs of five-year-old twins, Kim-Cohen and coworkers found that maternal warmth, stimulating activities, and children's outgoing temperament appeared to promote children's resilience to socioeconomic adversity and deprivation. They also reported

---

* The international governing body of the Bahá'í Faith.

that such resilience was partly hereditary and that protective processes operate through both genetic and environmental effects. As a result of genetic and environmental influences, some children who grew up under socioeconomic deprivation showed cognitive resilience. Furthermore, 46 percent of the variation of cognitive resilience and 70 percent of the variation in behavioral resilience of children with socioeconomic adversity were attributed to the genetic effect, and the rest of the variations were attributed to environmental effect. However, it is also important to keep in mind that adaptive capacity acquired through education and positive family environment has an impact that needs to be further explored. It is also possible that environmental factors have effects on the expression of genetic predisposition or the genetic coding of a person.[45]

PERSEVERANCE AMIDST ADVERSITY

Hardship is an essential experience in the road to progress and prosperity. It teaches us about stamina and perseverance. Through strenuous exercise, muscles become strong. Likewise, through hardship and the tests and trials of life, we use our intellectual and emotional "muscles" to develop enduring strength. Without exercise, these muscles become limp or atrophied. As a result, people who suffer no hardship in life and who are constantly pampered are deprived of developing skills to handle life crises.

To cope with hardship, one needs to have developed patience and perseverance as well as the ability to feel joy and contentment in spite of difficult conditions. As Dr. A. Khavari points out, "Patience is the gatekeeper of impulse. It counsels contemplation rather than knee-jerk reaction."[46] He furthermore offers the following fable about the wisdom of patience in the process of transformation:

A man found the cocoon of an emperor moth and took it home to watch it emerge. A few days later, a small opening appeared, and for several hours the moth struggled, suffered greatly, but couldn't force its body past a certain point. Deciding to help it out, the man took the scissors and cut open the cocoon. The moth wiggled out easily, its body large and swollen, the wings small and shriveled.

The man thought that in a few hours, the wings would spread out in their natural beauty, but they did not. Instead of developing into a creature free to fly the moth spent its life dragging around a swollen body and shriveled wings.

The confining cocoon, the struggle and pain necessary to pass through the tiny opening are essential for forcing fluid from the body into the wings. The helpful snipping was actually cruel, stunting the development of the moth's wings.[47]

Struggle and suffering, therefore, are what we also need for developing our spiritual wings.

In the Bahá'í scriptures it is stated, "O Son of Man! My calamity is My providence, outwardly it is fire and vengeance, but inwardly it is light and mercy."[48] We may sometimes face serious life crises that, in their outward expression, seem outrageous and unfair. However, these crises may potentially be the source of a new inspiration or positive developments that will be revealed in the course of time.

BEETHOVEN: SUFFERING AND SUBLIME MUSIC

Ludwig van Beethoven was born and raised in Germany in a family of professional musicians. In addition to the musical genius that he possessed, he loved nature and social justice. The music that he created reflects these loves, a phenomenon that characterizes the era of Romantic music. Ludwig's father, who was Ludwig's first music teacher, dreamed that his son would succeed and become a child prodigy like Mozart. He pressured young Ludwig to work hard and practice music for hours at a time, and sometimes he would brutally, after long nights of drinking, drag his son out of bed either to practice piano or to play for guests.[49]

Beethoven showed amazing talent and progress and gave his first public performance at seven years of age. As he grew up, he composed many kinds of orchestral, chamber, piano, vocal, and theater music, but at age twenty-eight he began to notice that he was losing his hearing, and by age fifty he was completely deaf. This world-renowned and unusually gifted composer could no longer hear his own music and had to resort to removing the legs of his piano and placing it on the floor in order to feel the vibrations of the music. This process served as a substitute for hearing the actual sounds.[50] His masterful Symphony No. 9, for instance, was written during this period of his life.

Beethoven suffered from a litany of diseases that he himself called "an incurable affliction." These included infections, abscesses, bronchitis, rheumatism, anxiety, and bouts of severe abdominal pain and colic during most of the last thirty years of his life. In his later years, he also had severe pain in his eyes that caused him to avoid the light and bandage his eyes at night. These illnesses, in addition to his deafness, plunged him into such despair and depression that at one point he contemplated suicide. But even though his last years of life were "as hellish as his final music was divine," he decided to persevere and cope with his deficiency and illnesses until his death in 1827.[51]

Speaking of Beethoven, whom he met in the summer of 1811, Johann Wolfgang von Goethe, who was very impressed by Beethoven's ingenious talent, wrote, "I have never met an artist of such spiritual concentration and intensity, such vitality and magnanimity. I can well understand how hard he must find it to adapt to the world and its ways."[52] Beethoven's life and suffering, as well as his accomplishments, were reflections of his strong resilience in the face of adversity.

TERRY FOX AND HIS MARATHON OF HOPE

A modern example of endurance under severe adverse conditions was Terry Fox, a Canadian student and athlete who, at age eighteen, was diagnosed with a malignant tumor of the right leg. In March 1977, his leg was amputated, a shocking experience for a young athlete. During his recovery, he was inspired by an article about Dick Traum, a thirty-five-year-old amputee who lost his right leg but managed to compete in the New York Marathon.[53] This sparked Terry's imagination, and he decided to run coast-to-coast across Canada to raise money for cancer research. In April 1979, sponsored by the Canadian Cancer Society, he began his run wearing a prosthesis attached to the stump of his right leg. The 5,000-mile-long journey from the Atlantic to the Pacific Coast of Canada would be difficult, but he was determined and never doubted that he would be able to make it. He endured terrible weather, rock-strewn or hilly roads, fatigue, and many other hardships with courage and dignity. He was up and on the road every morning at 5 a.m. and would run basically on the strength of his healthy left leg.

Along the roadside, hundreds of people came to support him. His Marathon of Hope took him from Newfoundland to Ontario. As he was running through downtown Oshawa, Ontario, his parents, who had arrived from British Columbia, were standing among the crowd of people. When his mother Betty saw him, she stepped out into the crosswalk to wait. But Terry didn't see her. "Concentrating, fighting fatigue, he ran on until he was less than ten feet away. Then suddenly he spotted her. His head lifted and, not even pausing, he ran into her arms, smiling a big smile. Betty cried and hugged him again and again, and cried some more. Then they turned and Rolly (his father) came forward, clasping his son's shoulders and hugging him hard."[54] They hadn't seen their son for a long time. By now, thousands of people had watched Terry Fox running, raising millions of dollars for the Cancer Society while fighting all sorts of hardships, pain, and exhaustion.

As Terry continued his marathon in northern Ontario, his physical condition deteriorated, and he required medical evaluation. X-rays revealed that his cancer had spread to his lungs, and he was taken to Vancouver. His parents spoke of Terry's childhood and how much he had hoped to do something to help handicapped children. By the time Terry's heroic journey to raise awareness and support for cancer research came to an end, he had run for 144 days, covered 3,339 miles on the road, and had raised millions of dollars for cancer research. Before his death, Terry revealed that physicians had given him a 10 percent chance to live. He stated that if he were going to die of cancer, he would accept it through faith and belief in a loving God.[55]

SPIRITUAL PARAMETERS OF SUFFERING AND GROWTH

The Bahá'í writings illuminate the interrelationship between suffering and spiritual resilience in overcoming life crises. In the Bahá'í writings, suffering is perceived as a vehicle for personal growth and fulfillment. For example, 'Abdu'l-Bahá states, "the more sorrows one sees the more perfect one becomes. That is why, in all times, the Prophets of God have had tribulations and difficulties to withstand . . . Therefore I am happy that you have had great tribulations and difficulties . . . Strange it is that I love you and still I am happy that you have sorrows."[56]

Regarding the relationship between love and pain, one may wonder why pain should become a necessary condition for the realization of the attainment of love. The reason is because pain and suffering can raise human consciousness to a new level of adaptation and enlightenment. Love, however, is a deep emotional experience that connects the hearts, and it is a path to perfection. Such perfection cannot be attained without struggle and pain.

Any cognitive change and rise to a new height of discovery and distinction demands exertion and struggle with sacrificial efforts. An athlete who intends to be the best—for example, the fastest runner— must exercise daily and exert strenuous efforts to attain the highest degree of perfection. A warrior is not a hero until he or she is tested, and the battlefield is also a testing field.

Goethe felt that there was a contrasting impact on human behavior by serious crises as compared to minor ones. He wrote, "a great crisis uplifts a man, little ones depress him."[57]

Persecution, suffering, and martyrdom characterize the evolution of world religions, particularly in their early stage of development and expansion. There is a general pattern of tolerance and submission to the Will of God among the early believers of each religion. In the case of the Bahá'í Faith, Bahá'u'lláh reveals that the suffering His followers experience is preordained to proclaim the Cause of God in this new dispensation and, therefore, empathizes with His followers in their suffering. Moreover, He elucidates that one's love of God will enable one to resist the powers arising against him or her and to overcome any fear. The result is courage and confidence, as observed in the multitude of Bahá'ís who have experienced torture and atrocity.[58]

According to the Bahá'í teachings, the creative words of a divine revelation—as a result of their unique vision of life—can empower the soul, transform the heart of individuals, and create a new race of people. This transformation gives a new meaning and purpose to life, and it dissipates existential fears and anxieties, replacing them with tolerance and contentment. When the vision of the true purpose of life and its ultimate destiny is blurred with doubts and superstitions, individuals are no longer able to maintain that sense of security and forbearance at the time of trials and tribulations.[59] The creative words of divine revelation have inspired resilience and courage in many believers in religion, and this phenomenon has been observed throughout history.

5

Creativity, the Mind, and Mood

"The mind and spirit of man advances when he is tried by suffering. The more the ground is ploughed the better the seed will grow."
—'Abdu'l-Bahá

How can mood play such an important role in creating a monumental piece of music or an astonishing work of art? Is it the mind that, through neurotransmitters, evokes cognitive excitement that results in a creative impulse? How does a psychiatric illness, a pathology, contribute to a creative process?

Understanding the dimensional interrelationship of human reality (mind, soul, and body) can have an important bearing on our perception of suffering and creativity. A letter written on behalf of Shoghi Effendi states that "we have three aspects to our humanness, so to speak, a body, a mind and an immortal identity—soul or spirit. We believe the mind forms a link between the soul and the body, and the two interact on each other." The human mind and intelligence, devoid of the divine reality of spirit, can also have devastating effects on human society and on the individual. As John Milton, in his epic *Paradise Lost*, wrote, "The mind is its own place, and in itself can make a Heaven of Hell, a Hell of Heaven."[1] The human mind can also harbor disturbances as a result of illness; however, mental illness does not seem to totally eclipse the creative power of the mind.

MOOD DISORDERS IN FAMOUS FIGURES

One place to look for the correlation between mental illness and creativity is in the lives of "famous" people. For example, Felix Post studied the prevalence of psychiatric disorders among 291 world famous creative individuals. This was a retrospective study based on biographies of the lives of famous men in science, politics, and the arts. All these individuals were noted to have excelled not only in terms of their abilities and originality but also because of their creativity, perseverance, and meticulousness. Post concluded that, for some reason, scientists appeared to be mentally healthier than people in other professions. The result of his research showed that "scientists had the lowest prevalence of psychotic abnormalities, but even in their case these were absent or trivial in only one-third. The amounts of psychopathology increase steadily from composers, politicians, artists, and thinkers through to writers. Severe psychopathology, in the sense of interrupting work, requiring periods of rest and sometimes treatment, exceeded the incidence of less disabling disorders in the case of artists, composers, and writers."[2]

While Post's results show that depression may not affect scientists as much as people in other professions, it remains one of the most common psychological problems among artists, musicians, politicians, and others. An example of a famous statesman who suffered from this illness was President Abraham Lincoln. In 1841, about two decades before the American civil war, Lincoln, who was then a young lawyer, wrote, "I am now the most miserable man living. If what I feel were equally distributed to the whole human family, there would not be one cheerful face on the earth. Whether I shall ever be better, I cannot tell. I awfully forebode I shall not."[3]

Psychohistorians have speculated that Lincoln suffered a long depression, from adolescence to his death. He lost his mother at an early age, and his father treated him harshly. Beside financial difficulties and an unhappy marriage, the strain of a bloody civil war affected him greatly. He was often overcome by feelings of social inadequacy and guilt, and at times he contemplated suicide. In spite of all this emotional and political turmoil, he became one the finest statesmen and orators, and he has gone down in history as one of the greatest U.S. presidents ever to have lived. This evidence rebuts the notion that mental illness always hinders one's ability to accomplish great things.

Among the well-known authors and researchers in the field of creativity and mental illness who have made important contributions in the past thirty years are Nancy Andreasen, Kay Jamison, Albert Rothenberg, and Ruth Richards. Their research indicates that psychiatric disorders are more prevalent among creative artists than in the population at large, and

Andreasen, Jamison, and Richards explored and identified a link between creativity and mood disorders specifically in bipolar patients.

Bipolar disorder is a mood disturbance that is recurrent and is characterized by cyclical mood swings from moderate to severe depression or manic states. In the hypomania or manic state of the illness, the mental activities are accelerated and the patient experiences elation, a euphoric high, exaggerated self-esteem, flight of ideas, grandiose thoughts, increased mental and physical energy, expanded imagination, and irritability. The individual can also experience accelerated creative processes, such as painting and writing, and these activities can be intensified by relentless euphoric hyperactivity and irrational, indiscriminate, and inappropriate interpersonal relationships, including business and sexual interactions, overspending, and drinking. As these activities accelerate, the person begins to deteriorate and becomes increasingly dysfunctional, eventually requiring hospitalization. In the depressive phase of bipolar disorder, the opposite occurs, and the bipolar person feels a sense of doom and gloom, poor self-esteem, loss of interest, hopelessness, depression, and a paranoid perception of life. The person loses a sense of pleasure and motivation, feels depressed daily, experiences significant weight loss and fatigue, feels helpless, and may have suicidal thoughts.

Jamison believes that the creative productivity of the manic phase is preceded by a feeling of elation and euphoria. Does a euphoric mood therefore facilitate the emergence of creative thoughts, and, if so, does depression suppress the creative process? Not necessarily, according to Jamison's research. She hypothesizes that depression may have an important cognitive influence on the creative process by slowing it down once the manic phase starts to recede. Consequently, in contrast to the manic period, when a person wants to express many irrelevant, unrefined thoughts, the depressive period allows an individual to put his thoughts in perspective. The excesses of the manic phase are eliminated, and as a result, the person's thoughts are more structured and more easily understandable.[4]

One of the first scientific research studies on creativity and mental illness was carried out by Andreasen, a renowned behavioral scientist. She used structured interviews, matching control groups, and strict diagnostic criteria in her study of thirty writers. In her study, she found that twenty-four (80 percent) of the writers had experienced at least one episode of affective illness or mood disorder. Approximately 43 percent of these individuals reported periods of hypomania or mania. Interestingly, she found that both creativity and mood disorders were much more common in the relatives of these individuals when compared to the relatives of a control group of writers with no history of mood disorder. This finding shows that creativity may have a genetic component that may appear in individuals whether they suffer from manic depressive illness or not. However, other research studies suggest that the psychopathology of mood swings has a kindling effect on the rise or decline of creative work.[5]

In another study, Jamison conducted research on forty-seven top British writers and visual artists who had been acknowledged with distinction in their fields. Among these, all painters and sculptors were either Royal Academicians or were associated with the Royal Academy of England. Among them were also playwrights who had won the New York Drama Critics Award or other related distinctions. Additionally, half of the poets were represented in the *Oxford Book of 20th Century English Verse.* Jamison reported that 38 percent of her sample had been treated for mood disorders and that three-quarters of those treated had required medication (antidepressant or lithium) and / or hospitalization. According to her, in this group, poets were the most likely to be treated with medication (33 percent), and they also were the only ones who required medical intervention for mania such as hospitalization and more intensive treatment (17 percent). Overall, 50 percent of the poets studied were treated with drugs or hospitalization for mood disorders.[6]

Research based on biographical evaluations conducted on living artists and writers reveals a remarkable and consistent increase in the rates of depression, manic-depressive illness, and suicide among highly creative groups of individuals. Reports of these studies suggest that suicide in these groups is up to eighteen times higher than in the general population. Depression is eight to ten times more prevalent, and manic-depressive illness is ten to twenty times greater than in the population at large.[7]

At Harvard University, Ruth Richards and associates found that manic-depressive and cyclothymic patients (those having mood swings with lower intensity) and their unafflicted relatives showed greater creativity when compared with those patients who had no personal or family history of psychiatric illness. Hagop Akiskal and coworkers interviewed twenty award-winning Parisian and other European writers, poets, painters, and sculptors and found that recurrent cyclothymic or hypomanic tendencies occurred in almost two-thirds of the study group, while depressive episodes occurred in half of them.[8] The authors noted that the temperament of artists was a striking feature of the sample under study. While hypomania often facilitates creativity, severe depression extinguishes it.

In another study of 750 psychiatric patients in Memphis, Hagop Akiskal and his wife, Kareen, found that those with mild manic-depression were more likely to be creative artists. But the same diagnosis also appeared in excess among individuals in business and leadership positions. Therefore the authors suggested that creativity and mood disorders can also include distinguished people who are not artists.[9]

There have been many gifted and world-renowned musicians, artists, poets, and scholars who have suffered from mood and other mental disorders. Despite their disorder, they were able to leave an invaluable legacy of creative work to posterity. A few of them are featured in this book to highlight their contribution and to celebrate their creative work in spite of pain and adversity.

METHODOLOGICAL ISSUES IN THE STUDY OF CREATIVITY AND MENTAL ILLNESS

In evaluating the interrelationship between creativity and emotional disorders among writers, poets, musicians, artists, and others, a number of methodological challenges play an important role in the reliability of any conclusions that are drawn. Researchers have been trying to overcome these difficulties in order to present information as accurately as possible. Some of these challenges are the following:

- A lack of reliable psychiatric diagnostic criteria in sample selection
- Heavy reliance on speculation, biography, and posthumous and retrospective information for diagnostic impression
- Lack of a universally adapted definition of "creativity" and its measurement
- Flaws in sampling methodology and formulating results
- Lack of control group and inadequate study samples in some studies

- A tendency to romanticize the notion of creativity in disorders
- Certain lifestyles providing "cover" for deviant or abnormal behavior, such as considering a hypomanic state as "artistic temperament" or an "intense creative episode"
- Challenge of pharmacological impact on creativity
- Limitation on study of etiological and genetic linkage
- Use of nonprofessional assessors to construct diagnosis[10]

With progress in understanding the nature of creativity, as well as having a clear perception of mental disorders and their possible link with creative talents, future research studies will hopefully break new ground in terms of accuracy and depth of knowledge in this field.

SCHUMANN: MOOD AND SYMPHONY

The eminent German composer Robert Schumann was born in 1810 in a family with a history of depression and other mood disorders. He was intensely emotional, reflective, idealistic, and generous. At age eighteen, he had his first episode of what he called "madness." In his hypomanic episodes, he experienced an outpouring of joy and excitement and a sharp increase in composing songs. This intense drive to compose was particularly noteworthy in 1840, his great "year of song." During this year, which was one of the most productive periods in his career, Schumann composed over 130 songs, an accomplishment unmatched by any other composer in the history of music.[11]

Jamison noted that Schumann had an extraordinary ability to put his feelings into music as well as to express them in his words. In his own writing, he once depicted these feelings of joy and elation as follows: "I am so fresh in soul and spirit that life gushes and bubbles around me in a thousand springs. This is the work of divine fantasy and her magic wand." In 1841, another important year of accomplishment for him in symphonic composition, Schumann described his inner experience with these words: "I was born in a fiery hour, I wrote the symphony in that fresh of spring which carries a man away, even in his old age, and comes over him anew every year." His euphoric mood and ecstasy would, however, after some time, inevitably subside, and he would be overcome by a state of melancholic mood and despair. "And so it is throughout human life," he wrote, "the goal we had attained is no longer a goal and we yearn and strive and aim ever higher and higher until the eyes close in death, and the storm-tossed body and soul, lies slumbering in the grave."[12]

INTERACTION BETWEEN THE MIND AND THE MOOD: AN ANALYSIS

The interaction between the mind, the mood, and the creative process is a complex subject, one in which our knowledge is very limited. Researchers have discovered a close association between mood swings, more particularly between the mild state of hypomanic temperament and increased creative achievements. This interaction is puzzling. For example, why is there a high degree of creativity among bipolar individuals? Is it because this kind of illness frees up the expression of creative impulses differently in different individuals? How can mood play such an important role on the mind in creating a monumental piece of music or astonishing work of art? Or is it the mind which, through neurotransmitters, evokes cognitive excitement resulting in creative impulse? How does a psychiatric illness, a pathology, contribute to a creative process? What about the process of creativity itself? Is it based on changes in molecular biology, or is it based on psychological predisposition? Is it linked to mystic and unconscious inspirations beyond our understanding? What are the ethical implications of the link between creativity and the treatment of mood disorders?

Researchers have concluded that during the hypomanic state, emotional and mental excitement, racing thoughts, grandiose ideas, exaggerated self-esteem, and heightened emotional and physical energy provide a mental environment conducive to productive accomplishment. But as the condition worsens, so does the decline of creative work.

A survey of Robert Schumann's musical works and his mood instability shows a striking relation between his moods and his productivity. While he was in the hypomanic state, for example, he composed the most, but in his depressive mood he composed the least. Both of Schumann's parents, as well as a few of his relatives, were clinically depressed, and one of his sons spent thirty years in a psychiatric institution. In the state of depression there is a crisis of energy—both physical and psychological—and a loss of *joie de vivre*. Edgar Allan Poe, well known for his extreme morbidity of thoughts, his "insanely depressed" mood with paranoid symptoms and alcoholism, depicted well the moment of melancholy in his short story "The Fall of the House of Usher" with the following words: "During the whole of a dull, dark and soundless day in autumn of the year when the clouds hung oppressively low in the heavens, I had been passing alone on horseback, through a singularly dreary tract of country, and at length found myself as the shades of the evening drew on, within view of the melancholy House of Usher."[13]

Perhaps the flourishing of artistic or scientific capability during certain emotional crises reflects some genetic or psychological affinity between creativity and mental illness. Frederic Flach believes that "all creative acts entail disrupting an existing homeostatic structure and subsequently synthesizing a new, more adaptive one." He maintains that such a cycle is a necessary part of a healthy response to stressful events. Based on this hypothesis, Flach proposes that certain psychiatric illnesses may need to be reclassified as disorders with a psychobiological mechanism that can trigger a creative process. Kay Jamison, a university professor and gifted scholar who herself suffers from manic depressive illness, also writes that the illness can have positive characteristics. She notes, "where depression questions, ruminates and hesitates, mania answers with vigour and certainty . . . Extreme changes in mood exaggerate the normal tendency to have conflicting selves; the undulating, rhythmic and transitional moods and cognitive changes so characteristic of manic depressive illness can blend or harness seemingly contradictory moods, observations and perceptions."[14]

Richards and Kinney note that individuals suffering from mood disorders who have milder forms of the illness may also show the greatest creative advantages.[15] They note that the fluctuations of mood, states of elation, and flights of ideas observed in mild forms of mania may enhance creative art or writing.

Arnold M. Ludwig of the University of Kentucky collected and published a biographical survey of 1,005 famous twentieth-century artists, writers, and other professionals. He found that the artists and writers experienced two to three times the rate of psychosis, mood disorders, suicidal attempts, and substance abuse when compared to successful controls in business, science, and public life. The poets in his sample had most often been either manic or psychotic, requiring hospitalization. His research showed that they also were about eighteen times more likely to commit suicide than the general public. These findings were corroborated by Kay Jamison in her comprehensive biographical study of thirty-six major British poets born from 1705–1805.[16]

LINK BETWEEN CREATIVITY AND MENTAL ILLNESS

The relationship between the creative process and mental disorder has been studied and documented since the time of Aristotle and even earlier in history. A variety of definitions, concepts, models, and beliefs have been put forward to attempt to explain this complex relationship and its mechanism. One model poses the assumption that creative individuals who have a mental disorder are gifted and have a special ability. Another concept of creativity in this context is that such individuals experience an altered state of consciousness brought about through a spontaneous or artificially developed regression into a preconscious level followed by a translation of the experience into the language of art. Since creative inspiration and its expression can stimulate our mood and feeling, this model assumes that our state of mind and mood may result in thoughts and imagination that may be translated into acts of creativity, such as a poem or a musical composition. As Tchaikovsky stated, "Schumann's greatness lies on the one hand in his wealth of emotion, on the other in the depth of his spiritual experience and his striking originality . . . With the shadow of his insanity already hanging over him, this inspired poet of human suffering seemed incapable of finding moments of tranquility."[17]

Many of the cognitive processes that characterize creative writing also characterize certain mood disorders, and the conceptual styles of many writers and manic-depressives appear to be similar. However, the similarity of thought processes between the creatively gifted individuals and certain mental patients lies on the surface. At a deeper level, these thought processes prove to be quite different. Given these and other observations, the line between creativity and mental illness is fine and probably permeable.

The question of why there is a higher incidence of creatively gifted persons among individuals with mood disorders as opposed to the general population is very intriguing. Likewise, one may wonder why a relatively large number of writers, poets, and visual artists suffer from mental illness. A common ground between creativity and mental illness may exist in intrapsychic conflict. With few exceptions, most creative people are less productive during emotionally calm periods of their lives, and many artists argue that their contact with the core of their primitive selves draws out the energy and inspiration that they need. Regression to one's primitive self can be a risky expedition, however, akin to walking the edge between sanity and insanity. This psychological vulnerability exists among creatively gifted individuals in their pursuit of exceptionally creative achievements. We should also be cognizant of the fact that, despite all these observations, many people are both creative and mentally healthy. Indeed, as Neihart pointed out, "The creative process is a mystery. We can know about pieces of it, but we are unlikely to unravel all of it. Many questions remain unanswered. If there is a significant correlation between creative genius and mental disorders, how do we explain it? Do mood disorders lead to creativity? (are these individuals attracted more to creative activities?) or is there a vulnerability that accompanies creative thought? . . . Is there something about the creative process itself that over time contributes to disintegration?"[18]

POSSIBLE MECHANISM OF A LINK

One may wonder whether a link between creativity and mood disorders would be the result of biological and genetic changes related to mood swings and cognitive perception during the manic or hypomanic state of consciousness. For example, do the cognitive activities precede or follow mood changes? Goodwin and Jamison have concluded that "cognitive changes precede—indeed cause or facilitate—depressive affect. Similarly, many creative individuals and students of creativity assume that inspiration, creative ideas, and fluency of thinking precede euphoric affect." Therefore the manic mood does not necessarily facilitate an increase in the flow of a person's thoughts and ideas. However, evidence-based observations show that mood changes such as elation or depression precede cognitive changes in writers and artists, and this observation indicates a possible link between mood changes and creativity.[19]

Emotional turmoil, although it can take a heavy toll on the personal and family stability of those who suffer from mood disorders, may also be viewed as a factor contributing to the identity of performing artists, musicians, or writers. In fact, the potentially high productivity and creative work of these individuals during an elated state may counteract the stigma attached to manic depressive illness and may enhance public awareness of the nature of the illness and the importance of its recognition and subsequent treatment. Some creative people who are struck by severe mood changes or other forms of illness may fear that psychiatric treatment will impede, erode, or compromise their ability to perform as a writer, a leader, or a businessperson. This fear can be alleviated through public awareness and open dialogue about the illness and its treatment.[20]

TCHAIKOVSKY: DEPRESSION AND THE GIFT OF MUSIC

Tchaikovsky, the celebrated and well-known musician who through his genius of music would turn demons into works of beauty, suffered from periodic bouts of depression. In 1854, at age fourteen, his depression began when his mother died. From then on, his depression never let up for the rest of his life. During his depressive periods he would become severely melancholic with insomnia, and at times he suffered from psychotic symptoms. According to Richard Kogan, himself a superb musician and also a psychiatrist who has studied the life and creativity of Tchaikovsky, the anguish that Tchaikovsky experienced motivated the legendary musician to be more creative than someone who had not experienced such anguish. Kogan believes that many creative figures "use their inner torment as a source of inspiration."[21]

Tchaikovsky's depression was most likely a source of inspiration for creating musical performances or worlds of fantasy through which he could find an escape from the painful world of reality. Examples of this are his works such as *The Nutcracker, Swan Lake,* and others. These compositions revolved around worlds of charm, beauty, and grace that were the opposite of his inner world of depression. In his insightful analysis of the work and mental state of Tchaikovsky, Kogan, a Harvard graduate in the field of medicine, stated that "there is a profound relationship between mental illness and creativity." Defining the process of creativity, he further elaborates,

In psychoanalytic terms, primary processing is nonlinear, non-rational thinking. People who are psychotic engage in primary processing. Secondary processing is what most mentally healthy adults engage in in everyday life. It is more rational, organized thought. Creativity works best when there is a combination of secondary processing and primary processing. The state of creativity might be labelled tertiary processing, where there is a combination. [. . .] If an individual is too immersed in a primary-process kind of thinking, he or she may lose a logical structure that is essential for a great work of art. But people who don't have access to those worlds beyond may not be able to create. They are too logical.[22]

CREATIVITY ENHANCEMENT IN THE MILD STAGE OF MANIA

A state of mild hypomania can usually be discerned by certain symptoms, which lead to increased cognition and behavioral changes that enhance creative and artistic expression. These symptoms are as follows: significantly increased energy and talkativeness, inflated self-esteem or grandiosity, the experience of racing thoughts, unusually creative thinking, unrealistic optimism, or an exaggeration of past achievements. People undergoing such mood swings may also experience enhanced productivity and may often keep unusual and self-imposed work hours. They may also become more uninhibited and seek excessive involvement in pleasurable activities. Such activities might include buying sprees, risky investments, and reckless driving. People experiencing wild mood swings often have no concern for the consequences of such behavior.[23]

Literature shows that a large number of twentieth-century American poets had bipolar mood swings. On the one hand, such a link between poets and the illness, whatever the degree of its accuracy, may lead to an inflated diagnosis of this morbidity among some of the poets because of the extreme inclusiveness of the diagnostic criteria. On the other hand, it may lead to a reduced diagnosis of this illness in others because of the assumption that among artistic groups such pathology is somehow normal. But can we call such a mental condition a mental illness or psychopathology because of the accompanying elation and ecstasy if the person otherwise is aware of reality? How can we classify the role of inspiration and mystical experiences that are sometimes described by artists and poets? Can the dark side of illness and the bright side of the divine be two extremes of the same continuum? Is it correct that the creative act involves a regression to earlier and more primitive levels of the mental hierarchy? Goodwin and Jamison believe that from early Greek philosophers to the twentieth-century specialist—there is agreement that artistic creativity and inspiration involve, indeed require, a dipping into untapped irrational sources while maintaining ongoing contact with realities of "life at the surface."[24]

Many artists, poets, and writers feel that life crises and ordeals played an important role in their creative accomplishments. Some poets feel that their pain and suffering provide an impetus and inspiration for their creativity. John Berryman, a contemporary of Robert Lowell, wrote, "I do strongly feel that among the great pieces of luck for high achievement is ordeal. Certain great artists can make out without it . . . but mostly you need ordeal . . . Beethoven's deafness, Goya's deafness, Milton's blindness, that kind of thing." Emotional power has played an important role in evoking insight in creativity, especially among poets. Goodwin and Jamison state that, for poets, "emotion is the condition of their existence, passion is the element of their being . . . for emotion of itself naturally heightens all the faculties, and genius burns the lighter in its own flames."[25]

Some of the best-known poets whose works are studied today in literature classes throughout universities and high schools in the United States suffered from various disorders. For example, the eighteenth century, also known as the Age of Reason, raised a number of poets who were psychotic or emotionally disturbed. William Cowper (1731–1800) was a poet who suffered many episodes of depression, mania, and repeated mental breakdowns. He also attempted suicide multiple times. During the course of his life, he used his mental experiences—psychosis, terror, hallucinations, despair—to portray, in the form of metaphors, the life challenges and conflicts of ordinary people. He even courageously portrayed his own depression in his work, and he created a new direction in English poetry quite distinct from his contemporaries.[26]

In a review of major eighteenth-century poets,[27] Goodwin and Jamison noted that five of them who were manic-depressive are also represented in the *New Oxford Book of English Verse: 1250–1950*. This number of representations constitutes 25 percent of the eighteenth-century poets, and it shows a very high rate of manic-depressive illness among English poets. For example, William Blake (1757–1827), who was a great visionary, mystic, poet, and engraver among the eighteenth-century poets, had mood fluctuations alternating from despair to exultation. He was very likely a bipolar patient who also had extraordinary visions and visitations. One of his many impressive works, called "The Marriage of Heaven and Hell," reflects his state of mood and mind.

Lord Byron (1788–1824) is another renowned English poet who suffered severe mood swings and eccentricity, and he had several relatives who were afflicted by mood disorders and suicides. His great uncle was known as "Mad Lord Byron"; his father, "Mad Jack Byron"; and his maternal grandfather had melancholic disorder. With such a family background, Lord Byron was often in fear of going mad and referred frequently to the "curse of the Byrons." A friend of Byron described him as follows: "The mind of Byron was like a volcano, full of fire and wealth, sometimes calm, often dazzling and playful, but ever threatening."[28]

One of the most graphic examples of depression in the life of a poet comes from Samuel Taylor Coleridge (1772–1834), who suffered from severe intermittent depression and erratic behavior. Coleridge was also an opium addict and a heavy drinker, and he described depression as "viper thoughts, that coil around my mind." The following excerpt is from *Dejection: An Ode*:

A grief without a pang, void, dark and drear,
A stifled, drowsy, unimpassioned grief,
Which finds no natural outlet, no relief,
In word, or sigh, or tear[29]

Virginia Woolf was another well-known manic depressive author. Her husband described her relationship with creativity with these words: "I am quite sure that Virginia's genius was closely connected with what manifested itself as mental instability and insanity . . . The creative imagination in her novels, her ability to 'leave no ground' in conversation, and the valuable delusions of the breakdowns all came from the same place in her mind." She herself stated about her impression of her illness, "As an experience, madness is terrific I can assure you, and not to be sniffed at; and in its lava I still find most of the things I write about." This statement reflects her elated state of mood and her perception of the link between madness and creativity in that frame of mind.[30]

CREATIVITY IN WRITERS AND THEIR RELATIVES

One of the first scientific research studies into the possible relationship between creativity, psychological disorders, and mood disorders was undertaken by Nancy Andreasen and her associates in the 1970s and 1980s. They used structured interviews, research diagnostic criteria (RDC), and matched control groups for their research, and their initial study involved a group of thirty writers who participated in the University of Iowa Writer's Workshop. Some of these participants were nationally acclaimed writers, while others were graduate students or teaching fellows.[31]

The result of the Iowa study of writers showed a very high rate of alcoholism and mood disorders among the study sample. The results revealed that 80 percent of the study sample met criteria for a major mood disorder compared to 30 percent in the control sample. The control group consisted of individuals outside the arts who were matched for age, sex, education, and who met the same evaluation criteria. Andreasen acknowledged that because her study concentrated on writers, the results could not be generalized to other groups of creative people. Nevertheless, the finding that 80 percent of the writers in the sample had mood disorders—where 43 percent of the sample were diagnosed as having had Bipolar-I or Bipolar-II disorders—reflects a prevalence of mood disorders among writers that is much higher than what is expected for the general population (5 to 8 percent).[32]

The study also explored the family history of the writers and found that the rate of mood disorders in the writers' immediate relatives was much higher than for the control group's immediate relatives. The researchers also reported, however, that the immediate relatives of writers had a higher incidence of creativity than did the relatives of the controls (20 percent vs. 8 percent, respectively). Based on this finding, Andreasen suggested a familial association exists between creativity and mood disorders.[33]

It is overly simplistic to assume that mood disorders such as depression promote artistic capability. But in some people, these disorders may enhance or uncover inherent creative capacity, and sometimes repressed creativity may express itself during stressful life events or emotional crises. At other times, a mood disorder may suppress the expression of creativity because of the intensity of the illness or the inability of the person to engage in creative work.

CREATIVITY AND BIPOLAR DISORDER

Benjamin Rush, who was one of the original signers of the U.S. Constitution and a professor of medicine at the University of Pennsylvania in the nineteenth century, made the following observations concerning the relationship between mild manic (hypomanic) and creative states. According to him, the mind of the hypomanic sometimes discovers not only unusual strength and acuteness but also certain previously unexhibited talents. He wrote, ". . . The disease which thus evolves these new and wonderful talents and operations of the mind may be compared to an earthquake which by convulsing the upper strata of our globe (brain) throws upon its surface precious and splendid fossils, the existence of which was unknown to the proprietors of the soil in which they were buried."[34]

Richards and Kinney used a unique approach in exploring creativity and bipolar disorders. They investigated whether individuals or their immediate relatives suffering from Bipolar I (manic-depressive) or cyclothymia would show higher daily creativity than two control groups. The first control group was composed of a mentally "normal" group of people, while the second control group was made up of people suffering from other illnesses. The authors hypothesized that a genetic vulnerability to bipolar disorder was associated with a predisposition to creativity. Unlike Felix Post's research, this study was not aimed at any known eminent or exceptionally creative individuals. Instead, the authors surveyed the "Peak Creativity" of the entire sample based on the most original major enterprise of adult life.

The results showed that Bipolar I patients did not display any special advantage or disadvantage in their levels of everyday creativity. However, those who were cyclothymic or the psychologically normal relatives of bipolar patients showed a creative advantage. Based on these findings, the researchers proposed that optimal creativity may be achieved when there is underlying bipolar risk, as opposed to overt illness or a complete lack of risk.[35]

The implication of Richards and Kinney's research is that mood disorders—or at least having a predisposed risk to one—influences a person's creativity. Goodwin and Jamison have argued that this creativity can be a positive element to a mood disorder, depending on the context in which it is placed. In their work on manic-depressive illness, creativity, and leadership, Goodwin and Jamison noted that when extreme mood swings are removed from the "sphere of poets and historians and placed in the more modern, analytical clinics of psychologists and psychiatrists, [they] lose their association, however tumultuous, with growth, sensuality, creativity, and other positive attributes, becoming instead representations of psychopathology. This is, in many ways, understandable. Clinicians are called on to treat symptoms, not to mystify them, and clinical objectivity is essential to avoid the risks of overlooking or minimizing a patient's pain and suicide potential." Speaking of the seeming benefits of the manic phase of bipolar disorder, Kay Jamison, in her book *Touched with Fire: Manic-Depressive Illness and the Artistic Temperament*, writes, "Occasionally, an exhilarating and powerfully creative force, more often a destructive one, manic depressive illness gives a touch of fire to many of those who experience it. The melancholic period of manic depressive illness is a source of intolerable suffering, yet there is strong scientific and biographical evidence linking manic depressive illness and its related temperaments to artistic imagination and expression."[36]

This link between psychopathology and artistic or other creative abilities raises questions on the ethics of treatment for mood disorders. For example, would undertaking treatment for bipolar disorder be ethical if the treatment dampened the creative impulse associated with bipolar disorder? Would withdrawing treatment be ethical if such a withdrawal led to the deterioration of a person's mental and emotional stability and resulted in psychosis, mania, or suicidal depression? Perhaps there is a need for a realistic balance between stability through treatment and the ability to draw on creative potential. To achieve this balance, the science of medicine has much to explore and new treatments to discover—treatments that will hopefully one day harness the illness of bipolar disorder and, at the same time, leave the creative inspiration untouched.

In *Touched with Fire*, Jamison analyzes the delicate need for treatment for people with bipolar disorder and the unwanted result of the suppression of creativity in these individuals. She asks, if manic depressive illness and its associated temperaments are relatively common in artists, writers, and composers, and if the illness is—at least to some extent—part of what makes their work what it is, what are the implications of treating the underlying disease and its temperaments by suppressing this creativity? Jamison then relates the following anecdote about artist Edward Munch, who was hospitalized on a number of occasions for his psychiatric treatment. He stated, "A German once said to me 'But you could rid yourself of many of your troubles,' to which I replied, 'They are a part of me and my art. They are indistinguishable from me and it would destroy my art, I want to keep those sufferings.'" According to her, "Many artists and writers believe that turmoil, suffering and extremes in emotional experience are integral, not only to the human condition, but to their abilities as artists."[37]

Although current mood stabilizers may render life flat and colorless for some, they also save countless lives. Many patients with creative talents miss the highs of mood swings, and as a result, they become noncompliant to treatment and stop their medication against medical advice. For example, at one point in my clinical experience, I had several patients who were suffering from bipolar disorder and who were also artists and writers. One patient in particular was a gifted artist who had had many bouts of depression and manic elation. Her painting and other artwork were her main source of joy and financial survival. In the course of treatment, I noticed that her stability with treatment was punctuated by unexpected bursts of energy and productivity that were followed by depression. The dosage of her medication remained unchanged, and she pretended that she was taking her medication as prescribed. Her lab tests, however, revealed that there was a lack of compliance with treatment.

Subsequently she admitted that, knowing her hypomanic highs would boost her energy and fire her imagination for painting, she would secretly stop taking her medication for a certain period of time. She would feel high energy, experience insomnia and, in a bout of hyperactivity, would paint day and night for a few days. Then, because she had had many serious relapses in the past, she would resume her regular dosage of medication to avoid another destructive relapse. We discussed this dilemma at length, and she was kept on the minimum dosage of medication possible. She learned about the warning signs and symptoms of relapse and understood that withdrawal from treatment could cause this overpowering illness to incapacitate her. After agreeing to take the minimum dose of medication, she was able to function creatively and live with her fragile mood, and she was willing to consult and upgrade her treatment whenever her mood was about to deteriorate.

My concern was how to sustain her stability through treatment without adversely affecting her artistic ability. In some cases, this is no easy task. One has to weigh the risk of relapse and its serious consequences against artistic productivity.

CREATIVITY AND SCHIZOPHRENIA

An impression exists in the general public that psychotic patients are less creative than the normal population. This impression has evolved mainly because of the negative effect that psychotic illness has on a person's thought processes. In a study that compared a group of psychotic patients to patients with a simple physical illness, researchers explored the differences in creativity between these two groups. A preference for complexity over simplicity was used as an indicator of creativity to test the patients. The results showed no difference between the two groups of patients, and the researchers suggested that, in the patients with a physical illness, the stress of the illness probably diverted the attention of these patients when performing complex tasks versus simple tasks. The study also showed a negative relationship between creativity and mental or physical disease, and this would appear to indicate that neither psychotic nor physical illnesses influence a person's creativity. The sample was small, however, and there was no control group of healthy individuals for comparison. As Eisenman indicated, mental illness may enhance the creativity of some highly creative people but may actually hinder the creativity of less creative people.[38]

Creativity among schizophrenic patients is different in many ways from that of patients with bipolar or other disorders. Studies have shown that the artwork of schizophrenic patients, such as paintings and drawings, is often symbolic, fragmented, or bizarre. Some exceptions, however, such as the following case, are extremely orderly and structured, down to the smallest detail.

Martin Ramirez was a patient who suffered from paranoid schizophrenia and rarely communicated verbally. Most of his adult life was spent in a state psychiatric hospital in California, where he died in 1960. He was of Mexican origin and had no previous art training. However, Ramirez developed a passion for art after twenty years of hospitalization.[39]

He began to create remarkable drawings and collages on sheets of paper. When paper was not available, he would often gather scraps of paper and glue them together with mashed potatoes. He hid his drawings from the hospital staff, whose policy was to confiscate and burn such works in order to keep the wards clean. Although he was in a mute state, he was able to express himself in brilliant and uniquely creative works of art. In 1954, he presented a bundle of his artwork to Dr. Tormo Pasto, a psychology professor who in 1960 put Ramirez's work on exhibition. Ramirez worked in graphite with colored pencil and crayon. One of his works, called *Alamentosa*, is an amazing piece of artwork in the Phyllis Kind Gallery, in New York and Chicago. What is fascinating is that, in spite of his psychosis and muteness, he was able to express his feelings and thoughts in such an extremely well-organized and minutely detailed manner, unlike the artwork of most other schizophrenics.[40]

In this chapter, current knowledge and research concerning the relationship between mental health crises, such as mood disorders and schizophrenia, were examined and elaborated on. Although the majority of research studies have focused on writers, poets, artists, musicians, and scientists, creativity is also associated with people from other segments of society, regardless of their occupation, whose creativity may also be enhanced and stimulated when they are struck by mood disorders and other diseases and sufferings. What is important—and often ignored because of the anguish and distress of adversity—is that the darkness of suffering may also be accompanied by the light of creativity.

6

Creativity and Mental Illness in Accomplished Individuals

"The disease which thus evolves these new and wonderful talents and operations of the mind may be compared to an earthquake which by convulsing the upper strata of our globe (brain) throws upon its surface precious and splendid fossils, the existence of which was unknown to the proprietors of the soil in which they were buried."
  —*Benjamin Rush, cited by Goodwin and Jamison*

Is it possible that an enhancement of creativity following disease or adversity serves as a form of compensation? If so, why do certain conditions enhance this process while others seem to impede it? Perhaps we should take innate predisposition and talent into consideration as well. As mentioned in chapter 2, Richards and Kinney suggest that creativity might serve as a "compensatory advantage" to the risk for bipolar illness. To support this concept, they cite the heterozygote advantage seen in carriers of sickle-cell anemia, who become resistant to malaria. A controlled research study on children in Papua New Guinea also revealed that Thalassemia disease carriers were 60 percent less likely than other children of the same village to acquire severe malaria. This observation that people with sickle-cell anemia and Thalassemia—both of which are genetic blood diseases—can be resistant to developing malaria was first reported during the 1940s. However, a long time passed before such observations were accepted as fact.[1]

How long have humans been adapting to malaria through sickle-cell anemia and Thalassemia? We don't know, but one theory suggests that this process has been occurring for the last five thousand years. We should note, however, that the development of this form of mutation is not the same in different populations. Nonetheless, this process shows that biological factors in one disease may protect against the development of another disease.[2]

CREATIVITY AND MOOD CHANGES

Similar to the positive effects of sickle-cell anemia and thalassemia in preventing malaria, the compensatory advantage of creativity for people with mental illness may persist for generations and can lead to educational or occupational excellence in life. The association between bipolar mood swings and creativity raises a number of "chicken-or-the-egg" questions. Is this relationship a coincidence, or does the morbidity (pathology) itself predispose the affected individual to a higher intensity of creative work? Is this a form of mental compensation to overcome morbidity? Or do the stimulating effects of creativity—resulting in sleeplessness and overextending one's energy to accomplish creative work—awaken mood swings? Do genes and genetic influences play a particular role in higher creativity?[3]

In terms of creativity, wilder mood swings do not necessarily equal greater creativity, for research shows that among manic-depressive (bipolar) patients, those with mild mania or hypomanic states are much more creative than those with a severe form of the illness. Inflated self-esteem, elated mood, high level of energy, sharpened creative perception, and increased productivity are some of the prerequisites for the release of creative impulses, but as the manic state progresses into the acute phase, the intellectual capacity for accuracy and rational judgment deteriorate, while the emotional and physical energy continue unhampered until the patient, if left untreated, reaches a state of delirious exhaustion. This latter experience adversely affects the organization of thought and logic that governs the creative process, and psychotic thoughts—instead of creative ones—consume the individual.

One may wonder why, if bipolar mood changes are compensated by creativity, there is a high prevalence of depression among eminent artists and writers. This is because of biochemical, genetic, and other factors that predispose these individuals to depression. However, Kay Jamison has stated that, among writers and artists, some have the capacity to experience and tolerate extremes of emotion and "to live on close terms with darker forces." Anthony Storr echoes this concept when he writes that "Man's extraordinary success as a species springs from his discontent, which compels him to employ his imagination . . . discontent, therefore, may be considered adaptive because it encourages the use of the imagination, and thus spurs men [or women] on to further conquests and to ever-increasing mastery of the environment."[4] Certain individuals afflicted with mood disorders, therefore, are able to ride the storms of their lives and effectively deal with the "darker forces" that Jamison describes.

Perhaps joy and sorrow are linked, in some mysterious way, to a higher level of consciousness, a divine inspiration resulting in unique creative work in some people. Bahá'u'lláh, for example, in His mystic eloquence about the journey of the human soul in the *The Seven Valleys and The Four Valleys*, states that "The steed of this Valley is pain; and if there be no pain this journey will never end."[5] If pain and hardship are necessary for advancing to reach a goal, then perhaps creativity exists in conjunction with suffering as a way for attaining this goal.

GENETIC FACTORS IN MOOD DISORDERS AND CREATIVITY

Richards and his coworkers studied a group of patients and their relatives using a broadly defined concept of creativity. Instead of basing their definition on significant socially recognized achievements, they used the importance of originality. Their research was based on the hypothesis that a genetic factor in manic-depressive illness is associated with a predisposition to creativity that is greater among the close relatives of bipolar patients than among the patients themselves.[6]

Richards and associates concluded that overall "peak creativity" may be enhanced in individuals with a mild form of potential bipolar disorder as compared either with those who carry no bipolar risk (like the control group) or individuals with more severe symptoms of bipolar illness.

They also noted a possible heightened creativity as a compensatory advantage among the normal relatives of manic-depressive patients. Rosenthal stated that "it is quite conceivable that genes for creativity and mood disorder are transmitted together"; however, although this assumption is intriguing, it certainly needs further research exploration.[7]

In a more recent study Kiki Chang and coworkers reported that both adults with bipolar disorder and their children who also had that illness showed greater perceptual creativity as compared to the healthy control individuals. They also found that the longer the children were sick, the less creative they were. The clinical implication of this finding is that early treatment intervention may prevent the long-term loss of creativity. In other words, the longer the children with familial bipolar disorder remain sick the less they will be able to demonstrate perceptual creativity. The study also underlined a genetic factor mediating the transmission of the illness as well as creativity.[8]

CREATIVE CAPACITY AND MENTAL ILLNESS

Although recent literature underlines a link between creativity and mental illness, in the past, mental disorders were not well defined, and therefore the use of expressions such as insanity, mania, or melancholy in reference to artists may have had different meanings depending on the circumstances. For example, Socrates and Plato spoke of divine mania or inspiration in describing the emotional state of poets. This term was also not used according to the contemporary definition of mental illness, such as mania. Likewise, Aristotle associated melancholic temperament with unusual talent.

However, this association was not always meant to link genius to insanity, as not all melancholics were insane. During the Enlightenment period, for instance, a genius was perceived to be someone having a balance in mental functions, while during Romanticism, a shift occurred in the goal of artists: originality gained greater importance over imitation. Consequently, reason was deemphasized to achieve greater freedom of the aesthetic imagination. In such a climate, artists became more eccentric and linked their genius to madness to the point that Lélut, a French psychiatrist, claimed that Socrates "had a most undeniable form of madness."[9]

This "madness" was sometimes idealized as an abnormal but fascinating expression of artistic creativity. For example, Farnsworth states that "musical giants are all by definition abnormal, i.e. supernormal in the area of abilities . . . they do not appear to suffer to any unusual extent from psychosis. . . ." Frosch also cautions against the generalization that mental illness is present among creative people by stating that "the creative furor of a Mozart may on the surface look like mania, but is unlikely to have the same structure or meaning [as mania]. It grows out of thought and careful planning; it is structured and has a product."[10]

Cattell and Butcher, in their survey of the lives of eminent scientists, conclude that the typical scientist of genius caliber appears to be more introverted, stable, and less predisposed to behavioral disorder than creative artists. Hudson agrees with this view of scientists and refers to them as "convergers" whose personalities are strongly structured and controlled from childhood. He uses the term "diverger" to describe the profile of artists, whose personality structures are more "loosely knit" and show more emotional instability.[11]

Although the relationship between creativity and mental illness is extensively discussed in this book, it is to be noted that mental illness is not a prerequisite for creativity or vice versa. Indeed, a large number of creative people are free from psychiatric disorders such as bipolar illness, and many mental patients do not display creative talents. Many of the studies reporting on creativity and mental illness have focused on accomplished and famous individuals such as writers, musicians, poets, and the like. More research studies are needed to determine the extent of mental illness in the general population who are creative.

ALCOHOLISM AMONG CREATIVE WRITERS

Alcoholism and heavy drinking have frequently been observed among American writers. According to Donald Goodwin, of the seven American writers who had been awarded the Nobel Prize for Literature through 1990, five of them were affected by alcoholism. Among these, Ernest Hemingway also suffered from depression. Donald Goodwin elaborated on the following possible factors contributing to alcoholism among writers:

1. The lifestyle of a writer maximizes the opportunity to drink, and his frequent isolation minimizes the chance that he will be found out.
2. Writing is a lonely profession, and a solitary lifestyle is common among writers.
3. Environment and expectation of people also plays a role. In the early 1900s, the prototype of the male author was a hard-drinking, hard-fighting, "macho" individual.
4. It is possible that some writers use alcohol for its disinhibiting effects to begin a project or to overcome "stage fright" when asked to speak in public. Yet many writers acknowledge that heavy drinking adversely affects their work.[12]

EMOTIONAL CRISES AND CREATIVITY
AMONG EMINENT INDIVIDUALS

Many creative people throughout history have suffered from depression or other mood disorders, but they have been able to achieve greatness in their respective fields. Some noteworthy artists are Michelangelo, Albrecht Dürer, and Vincent van Gogh. Composers include George Frideric Handel, Gustav Mahler, and Robert Schumann. Writers include John Milton, Edgar Allan Poe, Ernest Hemingway, and Virginia Woolf. Some politicians who suffered from mood disorders were Abraham Lincoln and Winston Churchill, who used to refer to his depressions as his "black dog." Among scientists, Sir Isaac Newton was probably the most eminent scientist to have suffered from manic-depressive illness.[13]

VINCENT VAN GOGH

An example of one artist whose creativity appeared to be a compensation for mental illness was Vincent van Gogh (1853–90). Van Gogh, a renowned artist of the nineteenth century, reflected in his art a deep sense of life. He suffered from mental illness, and although in the past there was no consensus about the diagnosis, more recent literature suggests that it was bipolar disorder. He had a family history of mental illness, and several of his siblings (including his brother Theo) suffered from depression. His symptoms included psychotic episodes, anxiety, melancholic insomnia, and physical exhaustion. During the last few years of his life, he also abused alcohol and was a heavy smoker. In his letters to Theo, he would often complain of anxiety and express his fear of poverty, disease, and premature death. Ironically, this latter fear came true with his tragic death at age thirty-seven. In spite of his physical and mental anguish and suffering, he produced a number of impressive masterpieces of art. Many of his paintings reflect the bright or dark side of his manic-depressive or at times psychotic moods.[14]

The way in which his suffering was translated into art remains unclear. His bipolar mood swings may have guided him into a deeper insight into the mystery of nature and the universe. During the most turbulent periods of his life, he may have used his artistic talent and creativity as a therapy to transform his suffering into something positive and productive, as he was undoubtedly able to express the forces of nature in colors to enhance emotions and feelings. For example, one of van Gogh's most famous paintings, *Starry Night*, was produced during his stay in the Saint-Rémy asylum when he was between psychotic episodes. It reflects a feeling of peaceful reconciliation between the ancestral forces (turbulent mind) and the laws and cycles of nature.[15]

During his treatment at Saint-Rémy, van Gogh produced other paintings and landscapes as he was going through depression and psychosis, including his work *Wheat Field with Cypresses*. Another of his last works of art before his suicide is known as *Wheat Field with Crows*. The researchers who analyzed his work write, "The stormy black sky and the turbulent field are reminiscent of depression and mania. The crows, flying toward or away from Van Gogh may symbolize either danger or hopelessness. The paths may represent Van Gogh's past history, but also the alternative directions he could take at that difficult point in his life. With such an unreliable sense of direction, it would be difficult to find one's footing." These authors also note that in a letter ten days before his death, van Gogh wrote, "They are vast fields of wheat under troubled skies, and I did not need to go out of my way to try to express sadness and extreme loneliness . . . I almost think that these canvases will tell you what I cannot say in words, the health and restorative forces." Van Gogh would later die in Theo's arms, saying, "I would like to go like this."[16]

POLITICAL LEADERS AND THEIR MOOD

Among political leaders, Abraham Lincoln, Theodore Roosevelt, and Winston Churchill all suffered mood disorders, and they were all accomplished political figures. Lincoln suffered such severe depression that at times he was incapacitated with occasional suicidal thoughts. A few scholars have suggested that he suffered from mild hypomania, but depression was most likely the cause of his dark thoughts.[17]

Roosevelt has been described as a person with symptoms of hypomania, including extraordinarily high energy, frequent grandiosity, elation, and extreme talkativeness. He slept few hours and wrote or administered ceaselessly. Some estimates show that he wrote 150,000 letters and several books on subjects ranging from naval war to hunting the grizzly. He was rarely depressed and instead was chronically in a hypomanic mood.[18]

Churchill has been reported to have been more cyclothymic (having cyclic mood swings of mild severity). However, unlike many people with a cyclothmic temperament, he suffered severe depression during the periods between his elated moods, and he had a tremendous drive to work. Lord Moran, who was Churchill's physician, recorded that Churchill in his depressive phase would speak of "black depression" settling on him when he was in a melancholic mood. He came from a family with a history of cyclothymic mood swings.[19]

Although political figures, like others in society, can be vulnerable to mood disorders, some of the so-called symptoms—such as grandiose thoughts and talkativeness—are so much a part of the political lives of these individuals that one cannot easily label these symptoms as pathology. Likewise, some religious experiences—such as ecstasy, inspiration, and mystical experiences—have been misinterpreted by some health professionals, especially those influenced by Freudian ideology and psychoanalysis, as being nothing more than delusions. However, such behavior may be seen as profoundly spiritual experiences unless the person clearly suffers from mental illness.

7

Neurological Disability
and Creativity

"Why is it that all men who are outstanding in philosophy, poetry or the arts
are melancholic, and some to such an extent that they are infected by diseases
arising from black bile . . ."

—*Aristotle*

The human brain is a magnificent yet complex organ with many mysteries
yet to be unraveled. It is composed of more than 100 billion nerve cells,
or neurons. This huge mass of neurons has a network of 100 trillion
connections among them.[1]

Both mental and neurological disorders have been shown to be associated with increased artistic or other creativity. Crutch, Isaacs, and Rosen,
in their study of a patient suffering from Alzheimer's disease, noted that
the patient's artistic productivity continued unabated in spite of his
progressive mental deterioration. They reported that although Alzheimer's
disease had "blunted the craftsman's most precious tools," it had not
destroyed them altogether and that the patient's continued activity offered
"a testament to the resilience of human creativity." It also gives an insight
into the neurological basis of artistic creativity.[2]

In the sections below, we will explore various neurological disorders, their
effects on creativity, and the use of creativity in dealing with these disorders.

FRONTOTEMPORAL DEMENTIA (FTD) AND CREATIVITY

Dementia has generally been perceived to consist of a decline in cognitive
and other intellectual functions of its victims. But recent scientific reports
and studies show that some of the previously acquired skills and talents
can be preserved in spite of dementia. Demented persons have been
reported to maintain musical skills, painting abilities, and the capacity
to play cards and word games. For example, one report showed that a

businessman became an artist as he developed dementia. Surprisingly, his painting ability steadily improved despite a progressive decline in his cognitive function.[3]

The neurological mechanism of this development is unknown. Some emerging evidence suggests that patients suffering from frontotemporal dementia (FTD) experience an enhancement of visual or musical abilities. In FTD, degeneration occurs in the anterior part of the temporal lobes of the brain, while part of the frontal lobes of the brain are spared. The presence of healthy frontal lobes may account for an increase in creative abilities in patients with FTD. FTD accounts for about 25 percent of pre-senile dementia.[4]

Researchers have been exploring the interrelationship between FTD and artistic performance. Miller and colleagues reported that five patients suffering from FTD acquired new artistic skills (became visual artists). Four of the five patients had the temporal variant of FTD, in which the anterior part of the temporal lobes were affected but the dorsolateral part of the frontal cortex was spared. As a result, their language and social skills were devastated, but their visual skills were untouched. In the conclusion to their study of these patients, the authors stated that the loss of function in the anterior temporal lobes "may lead to the 'facilitation' of artistic skills."[5] This observation shows that patients with the temporal lobe type of the FTD illness may offer a window into creativity.

Miller et al. reported on a sixty-eight-year-old right-handed man with a twelve-year history of dementia. Previously he was a successful businessman without any interest in art. As of age fifty-six, he began to paint images. At age fifty-eight, his language and memory deteriorated, while he experienced heightened visual and auditory experiences. During the following years, he created paintings with increased precision and detail. Between ages sixty-three and sixty-six, his paintings won awards in art shows. At sixty-eight, his drawing showed odd-shaped, doll-like figures. During evaluations, he appeared remote and unstable with little facial emotion. He had heightened awareness of his environment and spoke extensively on color and sound. An MRI showed bitemporal atrophy of the brain.[6]

A report from the American Academy of Neurology in 1998 revealed that new creative or musical abilities may emerge in the face of steady cognitive decline in some patients suffering from FTD.[7] Neurologist Bruce Miller, who made this discovery, stated that about half of his patients with this condition showed some sort of visual or musical ability. The case he presented was a man who had been ill for years due to FTD. One day Miller learned through the man's son that his patient was an artist. The doctor asked if the father's work was declining due to the illness. The son responded, "No, it is getting better!" Intrigued by the son's response, Miller began to seriously explore the reasons for the father's artistic ability, as he had not expected such innovation and improvement of artwork in a demented patient.

Miller found that when this patient was in his early fifties, his wife had died, and he had become depressed and left his job as a stockbroker. Although he had never had any interest in art previously, he abruptly began painting. The patient developed an obsession for purple and yellow colors that was evident both in his artwork and in the color of his clothing. One of his paintings, which depicted a sailboat with vibrant yellow and purple colors, won an award at an art show. With the passage of time, his artwork began to show more abstract imagery. He gradually became profoundly demented, aphasic, and disinhibited. Later his artwork became muddled and confused, which indicated that his perceptions were distorted and deteriorating. Miller indicated that twelve of sixty-nine patients suffering from FTD showed new artistic, visual, or musical abilities, or they sustained such abilities late into the course of their dementia.[8]

Copyright permission: Bruce L. Miller (Miller et al., Neurology, 1998)

If patients with no history of artistic talent and experience develop this skill in the setting of FTD, then what happens to a patient who has been an artist and then develops such dementia? The following report responds to this intriguing question. Mell et al. reported on a fifty-seven-year-old woman who developed progressive aphasia and then dementia.[9] She was an accomplished artist with a master of fine arts degree, and in 1997–98, when she was having difficulties with written and spoken language, she produced some of her best pieces of art. Her history of artwork showed a remarkable evolution over the fifteen years of her slowly progressing aphasia syndrome and then FTD. Her impressive artistic progress coincided with a decline in her ability to organize class sessions and grade homework.

The authors noted that patients with FTD can develop new artistic skills in the setting of their illness. What is interesting is that these patients have no previous background experience in painting. But the above patient was different in that she was already an artist, and the illness did not adversely affect the evolution of her artwork.[10]

Copyright permission: Bruce L. Miller (Miller, cited in The Medical Post, 1998)

EMERGENCE OF MUSICAL AND VISUAL ABILITIES IN DEMENTED PATIENTS

Bruce Miller et al. reported the results of their study of twelve patients who suffered from FTD.[11] In spite of the deterioration of cognitive and verbal abilities, their musical and visual creative ability was maintained or even enhanced. For example, among their patients was a forty-nine-year-old right-handed man without previous musical ability who developed progressive aphasia and became demented.

This man previously was gifted in foreign languages and had received a master's degree in linguistics. At age forty-two he became withdrawn, changed his diet, and constantly whistled. He developed musical ability and composed musical songs about birds. Although previously shy, he became inappropriately exuberant, and at age forty-seven he began to experience memory problems and was forced to retire. Neuropsychological tests confirmed right temporal lobe hyperfusion, a subtype of dementia.

Another case was a seventy-one-year-old man with previously developed musical and visual capabilities. He was evaluated five years after he developed aphasia. At age sixty-six he had grown withdrawn, and at sixty-nine he showed difficulties in understanding certain words. At age seventy his reading and writing abilities ceased altogether, and his comprehension declined. Nevertheless, he was a talented musician and could compose moving songs, and he captivated audiences and continued public concerts until age seventy-one, even though his musical skills had begun to deteriorate the year before. Interestingly, he was also an excellent chess player and puzzle solver, and his interest in these activities increased between the ages of sixty-nine and seventy-one when he was evaluated. He, like other patients, was assessed with a series of neuropsychological tests that confirmed left anterior temporal lobe deficit (FTD).[12]

In FTD, selective anterior frontal and / or temporal areas are affected by degeneration. However, based on their research, Miller and his coworkers reported that certain musical and artistic abilities remain unaffected in a person suffering from FTD. By contrast, in many cases of Alzheimer's disease, the extent and type of neuronal degeneration of the brain is different, and artistic and musical skills rapidly dissipate. However, the decline of these skills or lack of enhancements of them may also occur in FTD patients. Nevertheless, dementia should not always be perceived as a relentless loss of all intellectual abilities. Moreover, visual and musical abilities should be encouraged in certain cases of FTD. Interestingly, certain unexpected behavioral improvements can actually occur following brain injury, as outlined above, and this phenomenon is referred to as "paradoxical functional facilitation." In the process, the inhibitory and excitatory activities of the brain complement each other in a complex way.[13]

OTHER NEUROLOGICAL DISABILITIES AND CREATIVITY

There have been others who suffered from different types of disabling neurological disorders. In spite of the devastating impact of these disorders on health and well-being, some individuals have emerged with phenomenal achievements that have surpassed the capability of countless healthy people of their time. A renowned scientist and scholar, Stephen Hawking, Professor of Theoretical Physics at Cambridge University, is another example of creative success despite a grave and progressive disability. He entered Oxford University at the age of seventeen and began to notice that he was getting clumsy in physical movements and twice fell without apparent reason. Later on, as he was studying and was also engaged in cosmology research at Cambridge University, his condition deteriorated. At the age of twenty-one he was hospitalized and underwent intensive tests. Finally, he was told that he had amyotrophic lateral sclerosis (ALS), an incurable motor neuron disease.

It was predicted that he would not live longer than a few years and that his disability would get worse. This news shocked the young scholar. His physicians encouraged him to pursue his research at Cambridge, which he did, and he eventually got engaged to a student and married. This was a turning point in his life, and it gave him something to live for.

He was employed at Cambridge University to work in theoretical physics. As of 1980 his condition had deteriorated further, and his movements were severely restricted, requiring nursing care for a few hours daily. In 1985, after a bout with pneumonia, he had a tracheotomy operation and required twenty-four-hour nursing care. His speech became slurred, and later he was no longer able to speak clearly. He was in a wheelchair and began to communicate through a computer system and a speech synthesizer (called an Equalizer) developed in California that allowed his communication to improve.

In spite of all of these ordeals, he has made significant contributions in physics, including relating Einstein's General Theory of Relativity to Quantum Theory. He has written several books and numerous scientific articles. His two most popular books are *A Brief History of Time* (a best seller) and *Black Holes*. He is a professor at Cambridge University with twelve honorary degrees and is the recipient of many prizes and awards. He has four children and one grandchild and travels extensively to different parts of the world for public lectures despite his severe disabilities.[14]

"LOCKED IN LOCKED OUT": THE STRUGGLE OF A PHYSICIAN

Any tragedy or affliction can be heartbreaking for a person, whether a scientist, artist, or anyone else. However, when tragedy strikes a person in the prime of his or her life, someone who is fully engaged in the healing profession and who has dedicated his or her life to the alleviation of pain and suffering in others and to saving human lives, the effect can be not only physically but also morally devastating. This situation requires not only endurance with courage but also a deep sense of faith and reliance on divine assistance. The following story of a physician who suffered from locked-in syndrome is a case in point. It calls to mind the following beautiful poem of Rumi, the Persian mystical poet and philosopher (1207–73):

Hear the reed's complaining wail!
Hear it tell its mourning tale!
Torn from spot it loved so well,
Its grief, its sighs our tears compel.[15]

The brain stem stroke referred to as "locked-in syndrome" is the worst type of solitary confinement, according to Dr. Shawn Jennings, a Canadian family physician who wrote about his experiences with a life-threatening illness in an inspiring autobiography entitled *Locked In Locked Out*.[16]

On a beautiful day in May 1999, he left home in the morning feeling fine and, as was his routine, visited his patients at a local hospital in New Brunswick. After having made his medical rounds, he left the hospital and headed toward his office in a car. Around nine o'clock he drove into the parking lot of his clinic. As he turned his head around to back up for parking, he felt a peculiar ringing sensation in his head with visual disturbances. He suddenly felt unable to walk and became very dizzy. He called his office and asked for help, as he felt he was going to lose consciousness. At the hospital, a CT scan and other tests confirmed that he had had a brain stem stroke. A clot in his left vertebral artery had blocked the blood flow through his brain stem, and he had slipped into unconsciousness. His prognosis was very serious. When this happened, he was forty-six years old and the father of three children. For twenty years he had been practicing as a family physician, had taken pleasure in his work, and had been loved and respected by his patients and colleagues.

The brain stem is like a canal through which the brain sends all of its messages to the rest of the body. Therefore a stroke in the brain stem is devastating. The cerebral stroke (or brain attack), which is a more common form of stroke, usually paralyzes one side of the body. But the brain stem stroke affects both sides of the body and commonly interferes with speech and swallowing activities. Usually the facial muscles are paralyzed while eyelid movements remain unaffected. Jennings writes, "The brain is left perfectly intact, meaning that there is no confusion or personality change. The survivor is left imprisoned inside a body with no movement . . . I felt so alone when I was 'locked in.' I would have been reassured hearing about other brainstem stroke survivors and how they felt."[17]

Most patients suffering from brain stem stroke don't survive, or if they do survive, most of them are significantly impaired. A few may become "locked in" with normal brain function but unable to move, talk, or swallow. Dr Jennings knew all of this information when he suffered his stroke. His physician told his children, "your Dad is going to live, but he will never be the same." Shawn came out of his coma after the initial crisis but was unable to talk. His eyes were his windows to see the outside world. He became a prisoner of his paralyzed body. He couldn't talk, but he could blink his eyes, and blinking became his initial way to answer questions about pain and feelings.[18]

While still in the intensive care unit, he had a strong experience of hearing loud classical music in his head, which later he wrote about: "At first I thought the fellow in the bed beside me had his music awful loud. I searched the faces of the nurses working on me for a hint of their reaction to it. How could they let music play so loudly in an intensive care area? It was getting too much! *It is the middle of the night and they still allow him to play the radio! I can't sleep! Doesn't anyone care!*" Later he realized that it was only he who was hearing this music that was always present. The music was repetitive, and whenever one song finished, it would repeat itself, which was very annoying. "I heard orchestration, with a predominance of violins. I marveled at how my brain could come up with such complex compositions. I imagined this was a side effect of the stroke . . . I supposed that a minor clot had hit the music center of my brain—wherever that is located—and excited it. It stopped after a few days . . . Why was it classical? If the music center of my brain had been triggered, it should have been rock, folk, or guitar music that was generated, not classical. I never listened to classical . . . Can our brains 'compose' this music on their own? Is it a phenomenon of a brain suddenly having no stimuli? . . . I have always been spiritual and this has only reinforced my beliefs. Was it heavenly music I heard? I wonder."[19]

Through rehabilitation Jennings was able to take some control of his left hand and began to type on a laptop computer. His book was the result of two years of constant typing with his left hand. His right hand, however, remained the same. Throughout his ordeal, he never gave up hope. He went through panic, fear, and hopelessness, and he was treated for depression. At times he even contemplated suicide, but he persevered and gradually came to terms with his paralytic illness. Love for his wife and children and faith sustained him, and he wrote, "love was the basis of my acceptance and also my determination to improve. It gave rise to such phrases as 'I don't know if I will succeed, but I do know I won't succeed if I stop trying' or 'any movement I gain—however small—is a bonus.' Love was the safety net I used if I failed. What more in this world could I ask for but love?" He believed that love for God was crucial to his recovery, since a year before his stroke, he had had the premonition that something was going to happen to his family, and a few times he shared this strange feeling with his wife. "These feelings were true. I believe God warned me. He was preparing me . . . I love life. I did before, but in knowing God, it is even grander, despite my wheelchair."[20]

Dr. Jennings regained his sense of humor, and his faith in God grew stronger. His wife, a nurse whom he deeply loved, stood by him all along and gave him strength and hope. After almost one year of being treated at the hospital and rehabilitation center, he came home with his wife and said, "This is my life. I pivoted out of my car with Jill's (his wife) help, realizing that this was only a new beginning. Life would be different, but that didn't exclude fun, laughter and love."[21] Dr. Jennings's long endurance to go through this ordeal with faith and hope is an example of how creativity can help in coping with life crisis.

RISING ABOVE HANDICAP: DR. JACQUES VOYER

The following is an account of another physician whose perseverance drew much admiration after a critical injury left him crippled and in a wheelchair. He dedicated his life to the treatment of countless patients despite severe limitations. Dr. Jacques Voyer, an accomplished psychiatrist and a colleague of mine in Montreal, had been quadriplegic since the age of twenty-one when he was heading into his third year of medical school at Laval University. On a summer day in July 1970, he was swimming at a friend's swimming pool. He dove off the springboard and into the pool. His head struck the bottom, and the impact fractured a vertebra and severed his spinal cord, resulting in a quadriplegic condition. He spent a year in rehabilitation, and during this darkest time of his life, he wrote, "I had the most intense feelings of fear, shame, helplessness- and hopelessness. My life seemed over." With time and patience, and through the love and support of his family and friends, he found the hope and courage to continue his life. He came to realize that patience is a particularly important virtue for severely handicapped individuals, who have to rely on others for almost everything requiring the movement of their limbs. Two years later, still in a wheelchair, he had recovered sufficiently to resume and complete his medical education, although he had to abandon his dream of becoming a surgeon. Instead he studied psychiatry, and in the 1980s he married and began a distinguished career. He taught at McGill University and the Université du Québec in Montreal and wrote a book titled *Que Freud me pardonne!* ("Forgive me Freud"). It was basically his life story told with insight and humor. His message, based on the old saying, was "it isn't the kind of sickness a person has that matters, but rather the kind of person who has the sickness." He believed that attitude plays an important role in dealing effectively with the challenges of physical or psychological trauma.[22]

Dr. Voyer was an enlightened humanist who not only had to accept his handicap but, more importantly, had to accept himself. Such a handicap is "divine grace," he said. He evolved through pain and suffering and became a creative professional. Later on, looking back at what happened and what followed, he remarked that the event had made him a better person in some ways.[23]

EPILEPSY AND CREATIVITY: DOSTOEVSKY

There have been a number of highly creative people in history who suffered from epilepsy or similar syndromes. The diagnosis of epilepsy in these individuals was based on biographical information and retrospective analysis. The following are some of these individuals who were also considered to be highly creative in spite of their illness: Pythagoras, Aristotle, Alexander the Great, Hannibal, Julius Caesar, Dante, Napoleon Bonaparte, Jonathan Swift, George Frideric Handel, Jean-Jacques Rousseau, Ludwig von Beethoven, Sir Walter Scott, Fyodor Dostoevsky, Vincent van Gogh, Lord Byron, Percy Bysshe Shelley, Edgar Allan Poe, Alfred Lord Tennyson, Charles Dickens, Lewis Carroll, Peter Tchaikovsky, and Truman Capote. However, the current view of experts in the diagnosis of epilepsy confirms that only three of them had this illness, based on available evidence of symptoms. These are Julius Caesar, Napoleon, and Dostoevsky. In the past, diagnosis of epilepsy was overinclusive—that is to say, some people who had a few symptoms were not truly epileptic but were classified as having had this disease.[24]

Fyodor Mihailovich Dostoevsky, an epilepsy sufferer, was one of the most impressive novelists, journalists, and short-story writers in the history of Russia. Recurrent seizures began at a young age and were frightening experiences for him. Born in Moscow in 1821, he had an episode of auditory hallucinations when he was seven. In 1837, he lost his mother and in the same year had a "nervous breakdown." Two years later his father died. He was trained as a naval engineer, but during his work for the Ministry of War, he concentrated on literature. He had a tumultuous life that included violent epileptic seizures, a passion for gambling, and tragic losses and imprisonment in 1849 when he was sentenced to death because of his involvement with a revolutionary movement. A moment before his execution, his death sentence was commuted to deportation to Siberia. Terrible times in Siberia complicated his epileptic seizures and stabbing headaches. But his exile to Siberia also provided him with the opportunity to become familiar with people from diverse social conditions. Once he wrote, "There is only one thing that I dread: not to be worthy of my sufferings."[25]

After his release from prison, he traveled to Europe in 1862 and discovered the "corrupted" nature of western Europeans. He had profound insight into the philosophical, psychological, and religious conditions of human nature and society, and his writing flourished despite troubling bouts of epilepsy. Beset by financial hardship, he was compelled to write novels, including *The Gambler* and later *The Idiot* and *The Possessed*. During these years, in addition to enduring his epileptic seizures, he also suffered a bout of depression. His last great literary work was *The Brothers Karamazov,* which he completed before he died in 1892.[26]

It is not clear how much Dostoevsky's epileptic seizures, his imprisonment, and his deep interest in human conditions before and during his exile in Siberia contributed to his passion and extraordinary literary capability. He admitted that, just before the onslaught of a seizure, he would have an ecstatic experience. However, witnesses reported that his facial expressions in reaction to the impending seizure suggested fear and agitation. Despite his anxiety that he might lose his memory due to epilepsy, his literary capability remained intact. Interestingly, in his novel *The Idiot,* there are six epileptic characters, the most important of which is Prince Myshkin, the idiot who had ecstatic auras immediately before the outbreak of a seizure.[27]

CHRISTOPHER REEVE: VICTORY OF MIND OVER BODY

The life of "Superman" actor Christopher Reeve, who became a real-life hero after he was struck by tragedy, is another example of someone who overcame a severe physical handicap to become an inspiration to many. In May 1995, while engaged in his favorite sport—horseback riding—he fell and seriously injured his spinal cord. The accident rendered the then forty-two-year-old athletic actor a quadriplegic for the rest of his life, confining him to a ventilator and a wheelchair. Initially, he contemplated suicide, but later he titled his second memoir *Nothing Is Impossible* and worked hard to prove this point. During the first few years of his injury, he was impatient. Much later, in an interview several weeks before his death, he commented, "I remember telling a neurosurgeon 'Don't give me too much information, because at the moment my ignorance is my best asset.' Then, over time, as you learn more about the complexities of the central nervous system, and you learn to balance your life—even to get a life back—your perspective changes."[28]

In 2000, Reeve managed to move one of his index fingers and breathe for longer periods of time without a ventilator. Two years later, he stunned the medical world with the news that he had regained sensation in over 70 percent of his body and could also move most of his joints under water. His physicians attributed his progress to long hours of assisted exercise and a program of electrical stimulation that causes rhythmic contractions of muscles and allows for some limited movement.[29]

He did not belong to any religion until the age of fifty-two, when he joined the Unitarian Church. When he was asked what had caused him to change his perspective, he responded that it was because religion gave him "a moral compass." He also acknowledged that what really kept him going was the love and support he continued to receive from his family and the fact that he felt "needed." He wrote and published a remarkable story about Brooke Ellison, a woman who suffered a severe spinal cord injury early in her life. She was able to cope creatively with her injury and graduated from Harvard University with honors in 2000. Reeve believed that his work on the Brooke Ellison story was an important accomplishment in raising awareness about spinal cord injury and disabilities.[30]

Earlier in his life Reeve had graduated from Cornell University and was an accomplished pianist as well as an avid horseback rider. He had twice flown solo across the Atlantic in a small plane. Shortly after his tragic injury, he vowed that he would walk again by his fiftieth birthday. That milestone came and went in 2002. Although before his riding accident he was an accomplished actor and had played in seventeen movies and about a dozen TV movies, his real legacy may turn out to be his role as a tireless campaigner to support the scientific research in spinal cord paralysis. Within a month of his injury, he became active in advocacy groups and eventually established the Christopher Reeve Paralysis Foundation for spinal cord research. Through his efforts in raising substantial funds, he helped accelerate paralysis research and became an inspiration to a nation. He spoke at many occasions, offered hope to those who suffered from paralysis, and defended stem cell research for treatment of spinal cord injuries. Despite all his difficulties in achieving recovery from his own accident, he turned to the power of exercise and offered his body for exploring new treatments. Although he could not walk again, he inspired hope and perseverance and fought his paralysis to the end. In October 2004, he died of heart failure following the spread of a severe infection from a pressure wound. He was fifty-two, and his family was by his side.

In an interview with *Reader's Digest* magazine, he stated, "Your body is not who you are. The mind and spirit transcend the body." When Reeve was asked how the accident changed his perspective on life, he responded, "I have more awareness of other people and, I hope, more sensitivity to their needs."[31]

SAVANT SYNDROME: COEXISTENCE OF GENIUS AND DISABILITY

Savant syndrome is a condition in which a mental or developmental disability coexists with an extraordinary creative ability of genius proportions. It occurs in 10 percent of those suffering from autism and approximately one in 2,000 people with brain damage or mental retardation. About half of known savants are autistic, and the remainder are affected by other kinds of brain and developmental disorders. According to Treffert and Wallace, savant syndrome is "an uncommon but spectacular condition in which people with various developmental disabilities, including autism, possess astonishing islands of ability and brilliance that stand in jarring juxtaposition to their overall mental handicap."[32]

The above authors, in their article "Islands of Genius," describe three extremely intellectually gifted individuals who also suffer from disabling diseases.[33] One is Leslie Lemke, who is blind, developmentally disabled, and has cerebral palsy. At the age of fourteen, he was able to play flawlessly Tchaikovsky's Piano Concerto No. 1 after hearing it for the first time several hours earlier as he was listening to a television movie. Moreover, he can play and sing countless concert pieces and improvise as well as compose.

The second is Richard Wawro, who suffers from autism and lives in Scotland. His creative art work, including crayon drawings he did as a child, have been lauded as an "incredible phenomenon rendered with the precision of a mechanic and the vision of a poet."[34]

The third is Kim Peek, whom the authors describe as a "walking encyclopedia." He is developmentally disabled and depends on his father for his daily basic needs, but he has memorized over 7,600 books and knows the highways and roads that run between each American city, town, or county, as well as their zip codes. He is able to identify most classical compositions and knows the date the music was published, as well as the composer's birthplace and dates of birth and death. His story provided the inspiration for the fascinating character of Raymond Babbitt in the movie *Rain Man*.[35]

Many serious neurological disorders that, in the past, doomed a patient to utter hopelessness and disability are now viewed as opportunities for discovering latent potential that, with the help of science and technology, can be realized. This shows that human beings are highly resilient and have an inherent quality to compensate for disabilities, sometimes with astonishing endurance and creativity. The very act of coping with the distress of loss or disability in discouraging circumstances is a noble accomplishment and an act of creativity.

CREATIVITY, AUTISM, AND ASPERGER'S SYNDROME

One of the recent discoveries about a disabling affliction that becomes manifest from childhood—autism—is the astonishing intellectual or artistic capacity among some of those afflicted by this condition. Prior to these discoveries, those who suffered from this illness were doomed to a life without hope. However, autism and Asperger's syndrome have recently been making headlines in scientific journals and public media due to breakthroughs suggesting the potential of intellectual and artistic capability. Autism or autistic disorder is known as a pervasive developmental genetic disorder that appears before the age of three. It is typically characterized by sustained impairment in reciprocal social interaction, stereotypical behavior, and communication problems.

In 1943, Leo Kanner characterized autistic disturbances by the inability to relate to people and situations in an ordinary way throughout life. People with this disturbance fail to develop language to communicate, lack social interactive skills, have an obsessive desire to maintain sameness, are fascinated by objects, but have good cognitive potential.[36]

Similar to autism, Asperger's disorder (or syndrome) is characterized by impairment in social interaction and restricted behavior. It is a type of autistic disorder that occurs without the clinically significant delay in the development of language, cognitive function, and self-help skills. In 1944, Hans Asperger, an Austrian physician, outlined the characteristics of children who had difficulty with socially integrating into groups. Their social impairment resembled children described by Kanner one year earlier, but in contrast to Kanner's description, these children appeared more intelligent and had well-preserved language. Both autistic and Asperger's disorders are more prevalent in males than in females (male-to-female ratio for autism is 4 to 1, for Asperger's, 9 to 1, respectively).[37]

In recent years, further research has been done on the creative dimension of autism and Asperger's syndrome. The concept of autism has been evolving in recent years, and new understanding is emerging about the nature and characteristics of Asperger's syndrome, which is a mild and high-functioning form of autism. Although autism is perceived as a serious affliction, medicine hasn't fully unraveled the cause and treatment of this disease.

A growing body of scientific literature also suggests an unusually high presence of creativity among patients with Asperger's syndrome. Michael Fitzgerald, in his book *Autism and Creativity*, explored possible links between creativity and the high functioning of six eminent men in history who were perceived as having autism / Asperger's syndrome. He analyzed the lives and achievements of these individuals, but his definition of the autistic spectrum was very broad and overinclusive. In another book, *Genius Genes*, Fitzgerald and Brendan O'Brien correlate the achievements and biographical information of twenty-one famous and highly accomplished historical figures to autism, Asperger's syndrome, and an "autistic mind-style." The authors believe that these disorders contributed to the unusual and ingenious accomplishments of these prominent personalities and showed clearly the role of genetics in the expression of genius in this population.[38]

Establishing a diagnosis based on the biographical notes or documents of the past does not necessarily constitute a reliable clinical diagnosis, however. For example, solitary life, isolation, poor social interaction, and withdrawn behavior can be observed in many who have been deeply involved in research projects or are basically very shy people. These people may not necessarily show other characteristics of autism. The authors believe that a specific genetic makeup is a prerequisite for the development of genius and autistic creativity. However, they fail to take into account the impact of environmental forces in the development of a high level of creativity. Such environmental forces might include education, culture, life events, and nutrition, for example. This does not mean that genes do not influence a person's creative ability; however, we must remember that most behaviors result from a balance between the influences of nature and nurture.

The *New Shorter Oxford English Dictionary* defines *genius* as an "inborn exalted intellectual power, instinctive and extraordinary imaginative, creative, or inventive capacity, frequently opposed to talent." *Talent* is defined as "frequently, skill cultivated by effort, as opposed to genius."

According to Fitzgerald and O'Brien, creative individuals with Asperger's syndrome are "obsessed with fundamental, bedrock discoveries. They have no interest in being merely replicative . . . They get their 'psychological highs' on their breakthroughs in creative understanding. Creative work motivates them to do more creative work, to the last days of their lives . . . Because of their Asperger Syndrome, they are somewhat disconnected from the external world of human beings, and are therefore not so dependent on the approval of 'the crowd,' for whom they often have nothing but contempt."[39] Their disconnection from the outside world likely facilitates their concentration on their introspective creative endeavors.

In reviewing biographies and other sources of information for individuals with Asperger's syndrome, the authors frequently observed childlike qualities and immature personalities, which is not unusual in child prodigies. Because of their solitary, eccentric, and withdrawn lifestyles, such individuals can be inattentive or even distractive at social events. They can be oversensitive and fascinated by abstraction and logic as a way of creating order and control in the face of the unpredictable world around them.[40]

WILLIAMS SYNDROME AND CREATIVITY

Another neurodevelopmental disorder with emerging creative potential—different from autism and Asperger's syndrome—is Williams syndrome. What is interesting in patients with Williams syndrome is that, although they suffer from serious cognitive deficiencies, they are gifted with musical or other capabilities. Williams syndrome is a type of neurodevelopmental genetic disorder that is characterized by substantial impairment of cognitive function such as reasoning, arithmetic capability, and spatial cognition, as well as other highs and lows of mental functions. But in spite of these deficiencies, those suffering from this rare illness possess relatively preserved social skills, language skills, and musical ability.[41]

Levitin et al. reported a comprehensive survey on musical behavior of 118 persons with Williams syndrome (mean age 20.4 years) compared to an equal number of normal individuals (normal control group), as well as two smaller groups of individuals with other neurodevelopmental genetic disorders (thirty with autism, forty with Down's syndrome). Their study showed that those with Williams syndrome manifested a higher degree of musical accomplishment, engagement, and interest in social interaction than either of the comparison groups. The Williams syndrome group also displayed greater emotional response to music and interest in music at an earlier age.[42]

This is a very important and promising finding, given the serious cognitive dysfunction of those who suffer from Williams syndrome, a neurogenetic developmental disorder that occurs in approximately one in 20,000 births and is characterized by low IQ (ranging from 40–100). Such a creative and innate capacity in the midst of a disabling disease is a reflection of human potential for thriving amidst all odds.[43]

The presence of a hidden treasure of creativity in some of these distressing afflictions is encouraging. It may be especially comforting to parents of children who have autism, Asperger's syndrome, or Williams syndrome to realize that in the darksome presence of the disease and suffering, some patients may be blessed with the potential light of a creative nature.

8

Vulnerability versus Capability

*"O Son of Man! Thou art My dominion and My dominion perisheth not;
wherefore fearest thou thy perishing?"*

—*Bahá'u'lláh*

Vulnerability, in psychological terms, has been conceptualized as a deficiency in coping resources and capacity as well as an inability to fulfill commitment. Overcoming vulnerability involves a number of factors. Having a spiritual perspective regarding life crises can be an important element, as it gives meaning to life events. According to Lazarus and Folman, "existential beliefs, such as faith in God, fate, or some natural order in the universe, are general beliefs that enable people to create meaning out of life, even out of damaging experiences, and to maintain hope."[1]

Coping with life crises and suffering requires a shift of paradigm. One should reflect on the purpose of suffering and the new meaning it imparts to one's life. When we see our hardship in the larger context of global suffering, we don't find ourselves alone in suffering. This new perspective may give new meaning to our pain and enhance our ability to endure it.[2]

Breheny, in her book *After the Darkest Hour*, states, "when we take our suffering out of our dark isolation and see it in the larger context of life and stars and awesome powers, something important happens. We recognize the truth about our relationship to all of life. We are no longer alone . . . I look up at the sky and remember that the stars are present at midday just as they are in the blackest night—they're just harder to see." Sometimes we may find that larger context of sky, that universe within ourselves. If we reflect on it, we may discover the mystery of life. Bahá'u'lláh has written, "Turn thy sight unto thyself, that thou mayest find Me standing within thee, mighty, powerful and self-subsisting."[3]

Human beings are endowed with the paradoxical qualities of vulnerability and strength in relation to disease and environmental forces.

'Abdu'l-Bahá, in one of his talks, elucidates this combination in relation to spirituality:

The human body is in reality very weak; there is no physical body more delicately constituted. One mosquito will distress it; the smallest quantity of poison will destroy it; if respiration ceases for a moment, it will die. What instrument could be weaker and more delicate? A blade of grass severed from the root may live an hour, whereas a human body deprived of its forces may die in one minute. But in the proportion that the human body is weak, the spirit of man is strong. It can control natural phenomena; it is a supernatural power which transcends all contingent beings. It has immortal life, which nothing can destroy or pervert. If all the kingdoms of life arise against the immortal spirit of man and seek its destruction, this immortal spirit, singly and alone, can withstand their attacks in fearless firmness and resolution because it is indestructible and empowered with supreme natural virtues. For this reason we say that the spirit of man can penetrate and discover the realities of all things, can solve the secrets and mysteries of all created objects. While living upon the earth, it discovers the stars and their satellites; it travels underground, finds the metals in their hidden depths and unlocks the secrets of geological ages. It can cross the abysses of interstellar space and discover the motion of inconceivably distant suns. How wonderful it is! It can attain to the Kingdom of God. It can penetrate the mysteries of the divine Kingdom and attain to everlasting life. It receives illumination from the light of God and reflects it to the whole universe. How wonderful it is! How powerful the spirit of man, while his body is so weak! If the susceptibilities of the spirit control him, there is no created being more heroic, more undaunted than man; but if physical forces dominate, you cannot find a more cowardly or fearful object because the body is so weak and incapable. Therefore, it is divinely intended that the spiritual susceptibilities of man should gain precedence and overrule his physical forces. In this way he becomes fitted to dominate the human world by his nobility and stand forth fearless and free, endowed with the attributes of eternal life.[4]

VULNERABILITY AND EXPOSURE TO DISASTERS

The study of human response after natural disasters can sometimes provide clues that explain people's resilience during times of crisis. For example, B. G. Druss and S. C. Marcus have studied the impact of the September 11, 2001, terrorist attacks in New York. The goal was to know how Americans coped with these attacks by examining changes in the use of psychotropic medications in the weeks following September 11. They wondered, for example, if the shock and distress of the attacks was followed by an increased use of psychotropic medications by patients. If this were the case, they wondered if such an increase occurred nationwide or only in New York.[5]

They found that, in the general population, the severe shock and fear generated by the September 11 attacks were not associated with a commensurate increase in the use of psychotropic prescriptions. However, in certain subgroups of patients who had already been taking these medications, a modest but consistent increase occurred in the use of medications (such as antipsychotics) after September 11. The results suggested that any initial predictions of a drastic increase in mental health service use did not materialize after the September 11 attacks. This finding was consistent with previous research data suggesting patients with preexisting psychotic disorders required more medication in the face of crisis.

Hurricane Katrina—which struck three Southern states, including Louisiana, in 2005—caused a high mortality rate in the areas that bore the brunt of its landfall. A survey that was conducted by a group of researchers from Harvard University (Dr. Ronald Kessler and colleagues) revealed that, of the 1,043 survivors surveyed, a majority reported experiencing some type of personal growth as a result of their experience. The survey included assessment of anxiety and mood disorders, post-traumatic stress disorder, and suicidal thoughts, plans, and attempts.[6]

The researchers also explored aspects of personal growth that might have helped the survey participants to find positive meaning in their traumatic experience with Hurricane Katrina. Questions included whether the survivors had developed an increased emotional closeness to their loved ones, if they had developed a greater faith in their beliefs or religion, and if they had discovered a purpose in life or a form of inner strength they had not felt prior to their ordeal. When compared to the results of the previous survey of the people of the same region in 2001–3, researchers found that the rate of mild to moderate or severe mental illness doubled after the 2005 Katrina disaster. In contrast, the prevalence of suicidal thoughts was lower in the post-Katrina participants than in the pre-Katrina disaster. The reason for this may be that a brush with death can spark awareness of the value of life. Those who have succeeded in coping with trauma tend to view themselves as triumphant survivors who have not been victimized by life circumstances.[7]

What do these results mean? Why did people in the region have lower suicidal thoughts after the hurricane disaster? Perhaps the fear of death or recognition of a greater inner strength contributed to an ability to cope and rebuild life and helped develop a spiritual awareness of the meaning and purpose of life.

A large number of participants reported that they had matured emotionally after the disaster. On the basis of this result, one may conclude that the survivors of Katrina became emotionally and mentally stronger after experiencing the natural disaster and that this transformation caused them to have fewer thoughts of suicide than before. However, the low prevalence of suicidal thoughts might be temporary, and further follow-up and assessments are required.[8]

CREATIVITY AS PART OF THE HEALING PROCESS AMONG ARTISTS

As we discussed earlier, some artists suffer from depression, and their creative work seems to be nurtured and shaped by their emotional turmoil, isolation, and solitude. Their emotions find a creative way to express themselves. However, depression does not enhance creativity in all who experience it. In some people, for example, depression may lead to a desire to escape from the hardships of life, while in others it may motivate them to perfect their artwork. For artists who fall into the latter category, creativity is the inspiration that allows them to continue. Although depression is not an essential ingredient of creativity, many creative people suffer from depression. Not every sickness predisposes a person to creativity, however, and not all creative people are sick. What triggers an individual's creativity in the midst of a bout of depression is not known. It is possible that the incapacitating effect of an illness kindles a compensatory reaction that motivates the person to engage in an extraordinary adaptation to adversity.

Creative expression varies from person to person, and some individuals are more creative than others. This difference may be due to biological or psychosocial factors. Akinola and Mendes of Harvard University argue that "when individuals are biologically vulnerable to experiencing negative affect and are exposed to a situation that brings about intense negative emotion, they show the most artistic creativity." Although this is a possibility, it can not be generalized. An individual's background and personality must be taken into consideration. Personality traits of highly creative individuals that might have a bearing on this phenomenon are introversion, emotional sensitivity, openness to experience, and impulsivity.[9]

Being depressed and yet able to be creative reflects the dark side of creativity or dark creative energy. But it is to be noted that not all, or even most, depressive patients are predisposed to such a creative capability. Situational factors also play a role.[10]

Meana Kasi believes that, based on scientific observations, some people who are predisposed to creativity are also those most prone to suffer from depression.[11] The creativity somehow acts as a therapy for the artist, and his ability to direct his talent and energy to creative work may prevent him from falling into conditions such as addictions including alcoholism. Individuals in a state of depression should seek out treatment, but sometimes the side effects of medications such as antidepressants initially may interfere with an artist's production. Despite this drawback, however, antidepressants are indispensable in treating depression because, over a long period of time, they can help a person to heal.

Today, in many treatment centers for depression, patients are encouraged to express themselves through visual art, music, and dance. Such creative engagement in daily activities has a therapeutic effect and enables the individual to express latent talents and productivity that, in turn, raise his or her self-esteem and well-being. Such activity, however, cannot replace psychotherapy, medication, or other forms of treatment so vital in treating depression.

BIOLOGICAL CLOCK—ENDORPHINS AND PAIN

The pineal gland in the brain acts like the body's clock. Its function is timekeeping for the body, and, like the conductor of a symphony orchestra, it coordinates various functions of the body to ensure that everything is working together successfully. Its chemical mainspring is serotonin, a neurotransmitter (brain messenger) that is responsible for keeping a person in an upbeat mood. This biological clock has its own daily checking of the body temperature, sleep cycles, and stress. Other neurotransmitters are norepinephrine (for anger, fear, and fight-or-flight responses), dopamine (for pleasure), and endorphins, which are responsible for regulating our awareness of pain and stress. The discovery of endorphins has expanded our understanding of how we cope with pain and agony.[12]

Endorphin, the brain's own opiate, is a natural substance that is released in response to physical and psychological pain, stress, and suffering. Under certain conditions the endorphin level may rise, resulting in a lowering of the body's sensitivity to pain. In other circumstances, the endorphin secretion may drop, causing the person to become more sensitive to pain than usual. Endorphin levels vary from person to person, and the way the body will react to pain will differ from person to person. In other words, two persons exposed to the same painful stimulus may experience different kinds of perception of the pain. Although the mechanism of how we perceive pain is not clear, someone who is experiencing more pain will have a lower level of endorphins than someone experiencing less pain.[13] Severe stress causes depletion of endorphins as well as dopamine. A person suffering from bipolar disorder, for example, will have lower endorphin and serotonin levels during the depressive stage and higher levels during the manic stage.

Can intellectual stimulation, artistic excitement, or spiritual inspiration have biological consequences, such as a rise in endorphin levels and, hence, greater tolerance of pain and suffering? This hypothesis may very well be true, and it may help us understand the concept of individual vulnerability and resilience as discussed in chapter 2.

Endorphins were discovered in the 1970s when several peptides that seemed to possess natural analgesic properties were discovered. These substances collectively were called enkephalins and endorphins. Further research revealed that these peptides caused a reduction in a person's sensitivity to pain, even if the person was under severe stress or in a state of shock. Endorphins are believed to work by altering neural transmissions to decrease sensitivity to pain.[14]

As stated before, the quantity of endorphins released by individuals varies from person to person. Most often, it is released when we are under severe stress or great pain. Its secretion is also probably triggered by certain states of emotion and inspiration. Physical substances such as certain foods like chocolate and chili peppers may also trigger endorphin secretion. Therefore, some people may turn to comfort food such as chocolate during times of stress. This finding has had some medical implications in pain management. Acupuncture, massage therapy, and certain physical activities may enhance endorphin release. In fact, endorphin release may be responsible for the euphoric mood also known as "runner's high" and the "adrenaline rush" that occurs during vigorous activity.[15]

Furthermore, the beneficial effect of laughter and humor therapy may very well be related to an increased release of endorphin and hence its pain relieving effect. Norman Cousins, for example, applied laughter and a sense of humor to overcome his pain and disability (see chapter 4), and his experience calls to mind the statement of the great humorist Mark Twain, who stated, "The human race has only one really effective weapon, and that's laughter."[16]

These biological phenomena occurring daily in our life indicate our state of mind, our sense of suffering, and our ability to perform creatively under difficult circumstances.

MELZAK'S "GATE THEORY" OF PAIN

Ron Melzak of McGill University introduced a theory that explains the physiological mechanisms by which psychosocial factors influence pain. He believed that the severity of pain cannot always be explained by its objective or physical causes. Attention, anxiety, suggestion, and other psychosocial factors, for example, may influence the intensity of pain. Based on the research he conducted, Dr. Melzak introduced the "gate theory" of pain. According to this theory, signals coming from the injured or inflamed part of the body are modulated at the spinal cord level under the transmitting influences of the brain and other somatic inputs. He proposed that the dorsal horns of the spinal cord act like a gate to inhibit or facilitate transmission of pain impulses.[17]

As a result, an intense stimulation of certain trigger points of the body surface could decrease or eliminate certain kinds of pain. Likewise, certain psychological experiences such as attention or other intellectual activities might inhibit the pain by "closing the gate."[18]

Based on Melzak's theory, the mind—or anything that affects the mind—can play a role in inhibiting or stimulating the perception of pain. Psychological or spiritual influences, for example, may have a bearing on our perception of, and attitude toward, pain and suffering. Unfortunately, only a limited amount of scientific research exists to illuminate our understanding of human capacity for tolerance of painful experiences.

LOVE, CREATIVITY, AND HEALING

Love is a creative force that has important healing effects that have not been sufficiently explored. However, some studies have shown that marital life—particularly when love and harmony are present—promotes physical and mental health. Conversely, a lack of these elements will have the opposite effect.

Researchers have explored the possible consequences of marital conflict. One study found that in unhappy marriages, couples were much more prone to major depression when compared to those who were happily married. In a study published in the prestigious journal *Archives of General Psychiatry*, Dr. Janice Kiecolt-Glaser and colleagues reported that marital bickering can reduce the level of small signaling molecules (a chemical involved in transmitting information between cells) in the bloodstream, and this may sabotage the healing process.[19] The elevated level of these peptides, called pro-inflammatory cytokines, has been linked to delays in the healing of wounds as well as various age-related diseases including cardiovascular diseases, osteoporosis, arthritis, type 2 diabetes, and certain cancers.

Researchers recruited forty-two married couples for their study.[20] They examined an induced blister wound, which was carefully evaluated by a research team before and after low-intensity and high-intensity hostile interactions between the couples. A blood sample was drawn before and after each interaction for measurement of pro-inflammatory cytokines. The result showed a correlation between the level of hostility expressed by the couples and the level of pro-inflammatory cytokines in the blood of the participants. Less hostile participants had lower levels of the cytokines, and more hostile participants had higher levels of the cytokines. The researchers also noted that wounds healed more slowly in couples engaged in low- or high-hostile interaction as opposed to the control group, which benefited from a caring and supportive attitude in their interactions.

The healing of wounds in the highly hostile participants was particularly sluggish. This sensitivity of the wound to hostile stress and the elevation of blood levels of pro-inflammatory cytokines in hostile couples has important implications in physical and mental health. It also shows that loving support in marital life has the reverse result and may have an enhancing effect in the healing process. As Viktor Frankl notes, "Love is the only way to grasp another human being in the innermost core of his personality. No one can become fully aware of the essence of another human being unless he loves him."[21]

In traditional hospital treatment, nursing care with a compassionate approach contributes to healing. However, due to shortage of time and human resources, many patients today find themselves surrounded by machines and experiencing minimal contact with nurses and physicians. This dehumanization of medical institutions, if left unchecked, may undermine the very purpose for which the medical institutions were created in the first place.

CREATIVITY AND SEASONALITY

The role of the human biological clock and seasonal variations on productivity remains unclear, especially among those who suffer from seasonal mood changes.

Jamison conducted a study on outstanding British writers and artists in which she explored the rates of treatment received by a group of writers and artists.[22] She also studied seasonal patterns of mood and productivity in the same group. Participants in the study were chosen based on whether they had won at least one of several top prizes or awards in their field. Poets, playwrights, biographers, novelists, and artists were among the forty-seven participants who took part.

The writers and artists in the study were asked if they had received any treatment for their mood disorders. Thirty-eight percent of them stated that they had been treated for these disorders. Seventy-five percent of these individuals who had been treated had received medications or had been hospitalized. Poets were most likely to have received medication for treatment. Almost all of the participants in the study reported having experienced intense periods of creative activity. Fifty percent of these individuals reported that there was a sharp increase in their excited mood before the beginning of an intensely creative episode such as "excited," "energetic," "uplifted," "euphoric," "ecstatic."[23]

In the same sample of writers and artists studied above, Jamison explored the impact of seasonality and seasonal affective disorder (SAD) on the creativity of the participants in the study. She found significant difference in seasonal mood and productivity patterns between those with a history of treatment for mood disorder and those without treatment. In addition, the peaks of productivity did not coincide with the peaks of mood (mood peaked in the summer, while productivity peaked in the spring and fall.)[24] This subject needs further exploration to clarify seasonal effect on creativity.

According to Norman Rosenthal, well known for his pioneering work on the study of SAD, highly creative people with mood disorders are more likely to suffer from SAD than from other types of mood disorders. He noted that among writers, Emily Dickinson and T. S. Eliot were probably candidates for a diagnosis of SAD. Eliot was advised by his physicians to go to the south each winter, perhaps due to SAD. Among musicians, Rosenthal believes, Handel and Mahler were "most clearly seasonal," and both of them did most of their creative work during the summer period. For example, Handel's *Messiah* was completed during that time of year. However, a more vigorous and methodologically sound program of research into the relationship between creativity and SAD is required for a better understanding of this fascinating phenomenon.[25]

CREATIVITY IN JOY AND SORROW

Besides biological dimensions of growth, psychosocial aspects are intimately associated with two sentiments—joy and sorrow. It seems that both of these emotions contribute in different ways to the process of personal growth and maturity. Creativity is expressed in times of joy or sorrow. Both sentiments leave their imprint on the pattern of the creative processes in life. The interaction of pleasure and pain or elation and depression creates a unique experience of human consciousness. In the worst form it may cause a crisis of the self and a loss of human integrity. In a milder form, it raises self-esteem and potentiates a greater sense of well-being. Nature is designed to be creative despite all environmental hardships. In springtime a rose grows, blossoms, and brings delight to the garden. Yet in the fall and winter, it is stripped of its beauty and charm and makes a companion of snow and storm. Later, the change in season renews its life and the cycle continues.

PARAMETERS OF HAPPINESS

There are at least four parameters that describe the phenomenon of happiness: biological, psychological, social, and spiritual:

- Biological—happiness, or more appropriately in this context, pleasure, stems from the satisfaction of basic biological needs such as sleep, hunger, thirst, sex.
- Psychological—happiness that is the result of preservation of personal integrity, honor, personal achievement, and love relationship.
- Social—happiness that is a result of achieving social recognition for service to humanity and social good, noble philanthropic work, professional success and breakthroughs, and marriage and family relationships.[26]
- Spiritual—joy of drawing spiritual inspiration from establishing faith and communing with God, discovering spiritual truth and inner sense of peace and tranquillity. Recognizing that the ultimate purpose of life is to know and to worship the Creator.

These various aspects of happiness are on a continuum of joy from a very basic and elementary happiness to a more refined and profound form of spiritual happiness.

SPIRITUAL HAPPINESS

With spiritual evolution and movement toward a higher level of consciousness, the human mind and intellect should also evolve to a new stage of progress. Old habits and beliefs must also undergo change to be relevant to the divine reality of every epoch of human society. With the expansion of consciousness, individuals attain a new level of knowledge and behavior and new potential for action. One form of the behavioral expression of consciousness is the feeling of happiness or the experience of sorrow and suffering. Happiness as a process can be of two types as mentioned earlier. For material happiness, external stimulation and rewards are important. For spiritual happiness, the source of stimulation is mostly internal and relates to the inner human reality. Such happiness receives its inspiration from communion with the Creator. As a result, a person may be poor or devoid of material sources of gratification and yet be filled with joy and contentment. Those involved in mysticism experience mystic and spiritual rapture that may be incongruent with a joyless environment around them. This is another form of creative delight that stems from the mystic world of divine reality.[27]

SHORT BURSTS OF STRESS WITH BENEFICIAL EFFECTS

A short burst of stress may have a beneficial effect on autoimmune diseases and chronic stress. The brain and the immune system depend on each other in many ways. But under stress, one can drive the other to self-destruction. Patients suffering from autoimmune diseases such as rheumatoid arthritis, multiple sclerosis, psoriasis, and others, are sensitive to the pressure of stress in their daily life and particularly in their every move.

Some research studies have been aimed at alleviating chronic stress in this group of patients. Although rest and stress management are common approaches for coping with stress, recent research shows that autoimmune patients may benefit from a jolt of stress. In other words, it can be beneficial to fight stress with stress!

According to Dr. Andrew Miller of the Emory University Faculty of Medicine, "the key to chronic stress is acute stress." Strange as it may sound, Dr. Miller believes that short bursts of benign stress (e.g., a scary movie) may actually have beneficial effects. The physiological explanation of this interaction is very complex.[28]

Stress is believed to excite a trigger in the brain called the hypothalamus-pituitary-adrenal gland axis (HPA axis). This is the key pathway through which mental stress is translated into physiological activities. When one feels stressed, the hypothalamus in the brain fires a chemical signal to the pituitary gland, which sends another signal to the adrenal glands.[29] The adrenal glands then begin pumping out a variety of substances including adrenaline and cortisol. Cortisol interacts with the immune system as well as many other systems in the body. Cortisol and adrenaline help the body prepare for stressful situations by raising the heart rate and blood sugar. Through these interactions, cortisol calms the reactive immune system. The result is a paradoxical phenomenon: stress raises the blood cortisol level, and cortisol can control a raging immune system.

These scientific findings show that a short burst of a stressful event may end, at least temporarily, a lingering or chronic stressful experience. No doubt some of us have had this paradoxical experience in our lives. Sometimes the appearance of a major event stimulates a creative idea or insight to resolve or cope with a chronic problem. Although major depression is more than a chronic stress, nevertheless one may wonder if the use of electroconvulsive (electroshock) treatment has a similar effect in improving severe depression.

AN ANECDOTE OF UNRECOGNIZED POTENTIAL

During my residency training in psychiatry at one of the university hospitals in the United States, I observed a heroic and totally unexpected event in which one patient saved the life of another patient.

On a busy day, I was doing my rounds in an inpatient unit of the Department of Psychiatry, which was located in a building separated from the main university hospital. Suddenly a nurse ran up to me as the only physician in the ward that afternoon to say that one of the patients had had a cardiac arrest and had fallen unconscious. We rushed to the patient and, together with a staff physician, made every effort to resuscitate the patient without any result. In the meantime, the main hospital was called to send an emergency team, but because of some difficulties, the help could not get there on time and the patient, a middle aged man, was unconscious. In the same ward there was another patient who was an experienced surgeon admitted for major depression. He was always quiet and withdrawn into his own world. As soon as he heard the news, he ran toward our team and offered his help. He was mentally alert, and his responses were appropriate. After recognizing that all of our efforts had failed, he asked for permission to open the patient's chest and proceed with cardiac massage to revive the function of the heart. At a moment when there was no hope for the patient's survival, he succeeded. The heartbeat was activated and respiration resumed. About ten to fifteen minutes later, the emergency team arrived and the patient was taken to the intensive care unit. He survived and recovered completely.

As the cardiac patient was being transferred, our physician patient followed the emergency team to the door like any caring physician, calm and professional. Afterward, he took off the hospital gown and gloves, handed them to the staff, and returned to his room in the ward. In the ensuing days he slipped back into his previous state of melancholy and withdrawal. The intensive care staff's assessment of his timely and life-saving intervention was full of praise, and his work was judged medically well done. Had it not been for his immediate and efficient intervention, the cardiac patient would have been dead before the emergency team arrived.

It was an amazing experience, as none of us had previously thought that he could perform so brilliantly and switch so appropriately from depression to the mental state of a competent surgeon. When I told him later of the feedback of the intensive care unit and the fact that the patient had recovered, his reaction was one of great modesty. We learned that he had had other experiences of life-saving interventions of this kind in the past. Did a critical and near fatal crisis in a patient spark a sense of duty to save life in our physician-patient who had spent weeks in melancholic passivity? Obviously, it was not normal procedure to allow a patient to intervene in such a manner, but a jolt of conscience and this patient's amazing capability saved a life. Retrospectively, my impression was that he was suffering from a bipolar disorder, in a depression phase.

My observation of this incident in a psychiatric ward left a lasting impression on me. My perception of mental illness and mental patients changed significantly as well. I came to realize that medicine and especially psychiatry still are in a state of infancy: there is so much more to learn. Although one cannot generalize about this unusual case, I believe physicians and other health professionals should not underestimate creative potentials, which, like fire, are covered by the heavy ashes of morbid symptoms of depression or psychosis.

I also gained a new insight into patients undergoing psychological distress or suffering from the debilitating effects of mental illnesses. Although the mind may be impaired and unable to function for various lengths of time, the soul remains intact. The soul is like the sun, which, in the case of mental illness, is covered by the thick clouds of illness. The clouds may stay, move away, or periodically come back and cover the sun, but none of these will affect the sun, which will continue to shine above and beyond the clouds.

9

Suffering, Change, and Transformation

"In the darkness of the world be ye radiant flames; in the sands of perdition, be ye wellsprings of the water of life, be ye guidance from the Lord God."
—'Abdu'l-Bahá

REFLECTION ON THE SPIRITUAL AND RELIGIOUS MEANING OF SUFFERING

Suffering has been explored in different religious teachings that enable humanity to gain a deeper understanding of its meaning and its place in the journey of life. In Buddhism, to live means to suffer because neither human nature nor the world we live in is perfect. In Buddhism, it is believed that the origin of suffering is attachment to transient things and ignorance. Transient things include physical objects and our perceptions of these objects. Even the self is considered an object. The definition of ignorance is lack of awareness or understanding that humans have such attachments. Desire for worldly things forms the basis of our attachment and causes suffering. As material objects are transient, their loss is inevitable, resulting in suffering. Therefore, life is perceived as a process of suffering inasmuch as human nature is imperfect and impermanent.[1]

This analogy may in some way resemble the Christian belief that human beings are born sinful and that life with suffering is a cleansing process that ennobles our being. In Bahá'í teachings, human beings are born noble, and life is not a process of suffering, although suffering is inevitable. Attaining true happiness is a spiritual experience, not a physical one. In this sense happiness is life, and sorrow is death.[2] Attaining perfection does not always depend on the degree and duration of suffering. Perfections can also be attained through joy. In the Seven

117

Valleys, Bahá'u'lláh depicts the stages of evolution of a human being in the journey toward spiritual perfection.

In Buddhist teachings, cessation of suffering is attainable through *nirodha*, which means the cessation or unmaking of sensual cravings and clinging to attachments. This is one of the Four Noble Truths—that suffering can be ended through attaining dispassion. Human perfection and attaining dispassion has many stages and ultimately results in the state of nirvana, which means freedom from all worries and troubles.

The path to the cessation of suffering can be a gradual one, and it consists of self-improvement. This is the Eightfold Path, which is perceived as the middle way between the two extremes of self-indulgence (hedonism) and excessive self-mortification (asceticism). It is believed that this path will lead to the end of "the cycle of rebirth."[3]

In brief, the Four Noble Truths are as follows:

1. Life means suffering.
2. The origin of suffering is attachment.
3. The cessation of suffering is attainable.
4. The path to cessation of suffering.[4]

As psychology and behavior are in the realm of human relationships, they are implicated in religious teachings. The phenomenon of pain constitutes part of human behavior. There are three dimensions in the existential experience of pain: physical or biological, psychological, and spiritual. In biological pain, the pathway of pain experience is objective and depends on neurological networks that transmit pain to the brain's higher cortical system, which modulates the level of pain experience. There are a number of factors that influence the perception and expression of pain. For example, in some cultures, the expression of pain is suppressed, while in other cultures, it is exaggerated or intensified.

In the history of religion, depending on religious interpretation, pain and suffering have a particular meaning. In Judaism, pain and suffering are viewed as part of human fate and as the consequence of sin. Suffering is also perceived as a way to atone for sin, but the believers are not encouraged to seek out pain, nor are they to avoid seeking a remedy for it. The Christian and Islamic concept of suffering is based on the understanding that it is a means of punishment for sin. Like the Jews, Christians and Muslims are discouraged from seeking out pain or avoiding treatment for it. These experiences contribute to personal growth.[5]

Augustine (354–430) believed that health was something good that should be sought after, but he reminded Christians that God had promised them not health but rather eternal life in heaven where there is no pain, suffering, or fear. In Hinduism, pain is viewed as a defining characteristic of earthly life that is to be endured, while in Buddhism, the purpose of pain is to detach us from the material world, a world of pain and illusion.[6]

In the Bahá'í Faith, pain and suffering are seen as life experiences that help one strive for human perfection. Without these, one may not be able to attain true perfection, personal growth, and fulfillment. "Men who suffer not, attain no perfection," states 'Abdu'l-Bahá. He also says, "The plant most pruned by the gardener is that one which, when the summer comes, will have the most beautiful blossoms and the most abundant fruit." Bahá'í teachings also indicate that these difficult experiences will enhance spiritual growth and will deepen our understanding of the true purpose of life and its meaning. 'Abdu'l-Bahá has further stated, "The mind and spirit of man advance when he is tried by suffering. The more the ground is ploughed the better the seed will grow, the better the harvest will be. Just as the plough furrows the earth deeply, purifying it of weeds and thistles, so suffering and tribulation free man from the petty affairs of this worldly life until he arrives at a state of complete detachment. His attitude in this world will be that of divine happiness. Man is, so to speak, unripe: the heat of the fire of suffering will mature him. Look back to the times past and you will find that the greatest men have suffered most."[7]

According to this statement, advancement of the mind and spirit is connected to the experience of suffering. It frees the individual from the petty affairs of the world, from undue attachment to the material world. Although in a materialistic society, suffering is seen as a disease, a trauma, something to avoid, 'Abdu'l-Bahá clearly states that the spiritual outcome of suffering is something positive. It is possible that the more we are attached to material things, the more we may become susceptible to the tests of suffering. However, Bahá'ís don't seek out pain or suffering, nor do they believe that pain is the only road to personal growth and perfection.

What is important is to recognize the spiritual dimension of our life and view it in a larger picture of creation in which there is a meaning and purpose. 'Abdu'l-Bahá says, "Turn towards God, and seek always to do that which is right and noble. Enrich the poor, raise the fallen, comfort the sorrowful, bring healing to the sick, reassure the fearful, rescue the oppressed, bring hope to the hopeless, shelter the destitute."[8] Therefore the path to joy and tranquillity is found not only through detachment from worldly things, but also by having a spiritual perspective on life that will contribute to the well-being of society and the advancement of civilization.

CHANGE IS A CONSTANT

Change is an essential quality of progress in life. We change as we grow, and we grow as we change. Change can also be positive or negative in its expression. A seed expands and grows to become a plant. A plant is no longer a seed, although it is the fulfillment of all the potential inherent in the seed. 'Abdu'l-Bahá states:

> If you plant a seed in the ground, a tree will become manifest from that seed. The seed sacrifices itself to the tree that will come from it. The seed is outwardly lost, destroyed; but the same seed which is sacrificed will be absorbed and embodied in the tree, its blossoms, fruit and branches. If the identity of that seed had not been sacrificed to the tree . . . no branches, blossoms or fruits would have been forthcoming . . . When you look at the tree, you will realize that the perfections, blessings, properties and beauty of the seed have become manifest in the branches, twigs, blossoms and fruit . . .[9]

Likewise, a little baby grows into a child, an adolescent, an adult, an elderly person, and ultimately dies. But as one grows, he or she has the potential to become either a noble, peace-loving, true servant of humanity or to become a ruthless criminal. The outcome is largely dependent on the individual's education, childhood role models, and spiritual insight into the true purpose of life.

Breheny cites the works of an early Greek philosopher, Heraclitus, who wrote, "No man ever steps into the same river twice, for it's not the same river and he's not the same man."[10] As much as the rushing waters of a moving river are in constant flux and change, so are we in our own lives constantly changing. Those who can't accept the inevitability of change (such as a change in health, family life, or aging) may have to pay the price when there is no alternative but to accept. The ability to accept what is unavoidable and to adapt to it constructively is a creative performance.

Suffering has also accompanied major developments in the evolution of societies in the course of history. The following statement illustrates the depth and meaning of the tragic situation that the world of humanity is experiencing at present:

> Our world is passing through the darkest period in the entire history of civilization, in which unnumbered millions of people suffer grievous wrongs that drive them to the edge of despair. It is one of the mysteries of the spiritual realm that the destinies of those who have great contributions to make should entail suffering of the kind your letter so movingly describes. What we do know, beyond any possibility of doubt, is that these black clouds will lift, that the spiritual potentialities of those who are now undergoing such severe testing will find fulfillment and that the whole world will benefit.[11]

In the mineral world, the process of change occurs in different ways. To illustrate the purpose of change, 'Abdu'l-Bahá uses the following analogy of the transformation of iron from one shape or form to another through the influence of heat:

> Observe its [iron] qualities; it is solid, black, cold. These are the characteristics of iron. When the same iron absorbs heat from the fire, it sacrifices its attribute of solidity for the attribute of fluidity. It sacrifices its attribute of darkness for the attribute of light, which is a quality of the fire. It sacrifices its attribute of coldness to the quality of heat which the fire possesses so that in the iron there remains no solidity, darkness or cold. It becomes illumined and transformed, having sacrificed its qualities to the qualities and attributes of the fire.
>
> Likewise, man, when separated and severed from the attributes of the world of nature, sacrifices the qualities and exigencies of that mortal realm and manifests the perfections of the Kingdom, just

as the qualities of the iron disappeared and the qualities of the fire appeared in their place.[12]

When we reflect on our personal development as well as on the development of the world around us, we realize that change is unavoidable. But the manner in which we adapt to change is not without pain and requires patience and creativity.

CREATIVE INTERACTION BETWEEN CRISIS AND VICTORY IN RELIGION

The creative interaction between crisis and victory is a phenomenon that has characterized the evolution of each of the world's religions as witnessed in their history. It is evident from the Bahá'í writings that although opposition and atrocities against the Bahá'í Faith will bring countless hardships and suffering, they will also kindle a new impulse for its developmental progress. "The resistless march of the Faith of Bahá'u'lláh, viewed in this light, and propelled by the stimulating influences which the unwisdom of its enemies and the force latent within itself both engender, resolves itself into a series of rhythmic pulsations, precipitated, on the one hand, through the explosive outbursts of its foes, and the vibrations of Divine Power, on the other, which speed it, with ever-increasing momentum, along that predestined course traced for it by the Hand of the Almighty." The evolution and progress of every ideology or movement does not follow a linear path. It experiences challenges and opportunities and advances not in a uniform pattern of growth, but in surges characterized by crisis and victory. This is particularly true in the history of religion, where the assault of persecution fuels the development and triumph of a faith. Bahá'u'lláh states, "In the beginning of every Revelation adversities have prevailed which later on have been turned into great prosperity."[13]

The spiritual energy released through the creative Word of God is endowed with a potency that prepares the way for the dialectical process of expansion and consolidation of a world religion. This is like a drama played in the divine theater of the world of humanity that demonstrates the creative side of suffering, a suffering that is endowed with a purpose. The Universal House of Justice states:

Events of the most profound significance are taking place in the world. The river of human history is flowing at a bewildering speed. Age-old institutions are collapsing. Traditional ways are being forgotten, and newly born ideologies which were fondly expected to take their place, are withering and decaying before the eyes of their disillusioned adherents. Amidst this decay and disruption, assailed from every side by the turmoil of the age, the Order of Bahá'u'lláh, unshakably founded on the Word of God, protected by the shield of the divine Covenant and assisted by the hosts of the Concourse on High, is rising in every part of the world.[14]

BAHÁ'Í PERSPECTIVES ON TESTS, SUFFERING, AND PERSEVERANCE

Our perception of tests and trials largely depends on our own personal experiences as well as on the reactions of our family and our role-models to life crises. Cultural and religious beliefs about personal and collective suffering also have an impact on our minds. But in general, people have the tendency to perceive the dark side of pain and suffering rather than the potential for learning and growth that may result from existential events. Religious teachings view life crises in a larger context that gives meaning to life trials, the result of which can be to empower individuals to achieve personal growth. Adib Taherzadeh, elaborating on perseverance amidst adversity in the Bahá'í Faith, stated:

History has shown that many eminent men have achieved greatness merely by facing hardships and difficulties. Through perseverance and steadfastness they have overcome obstacles, demonstrated their strength of character and revealed the hidden powers latent within them. In contrast, the weak and feeble have often succumbed to such difficulties and perished. Clearly, suffering reveals the strength, the character and the faith of every human being. The greater the cause, the more strenuous are the tests and trials to which the individual is subjected. In this Dispensation, from amidst the blood-baths of martyrdom, great heroes have emerged whose lives have illumined the history of the Cause of God by their courage and self-sacrifice.[15]

In the Bahá'í writings, tests have been referred to as blessings in disguise or gifts of God that work in "mysterious" ways. Some tests are the result of our own behavior, while others are sent for our spiritual progress.

The human soul is endowed with a capacity that is far beyond our understanding. Elaborating on the distinction and independence of the soul in relation to afflictions of the body and mind, Bahá'u'lláh states, "Know thou that the soul of man is exalted above, and is independent of all infirmities of body or mind . . . the soul itself remaineth unaffected by any bodily ailments. Consider the light of the lamp. Though an external object may interfere with its radiance, the light itself continueth to shine with undiminished power."[16]

Recognizing the meaning of life crises and tribulation can help us have a deeper understanding of the dynamics of human transformations. Through the insight and learning that come from hardship we are polished and prepared for the life beyond this earthly world. The Bahá'í writings explain that "Suffering, of one kind or another, seems to be the portion of man in this world. Even the Beloved ones, the Prophets of God, have never been exempt from the ills that are to be found in our world; poverty, disease, bereavement,—they seem to be part of the polish God employs to make us finer, and enable us to reflect more of His attributes!"[17]

When facing an inevitable ordeal or crisis, 'Abdu'l-Bahá encourages us to acknowledge the situation with patience and strive to overcome the difficulties: "When calamity striketh, be ye patient and composed. However afflictive your sufferings may be, stay ye undisturbed, and with perfect confidence in the abounding grace of God, brave ye the tempest of tribulations and fiery ordeals."[18]

Having a positive perception of life difficulties can enable us to rise above our limitations and face challenges, but developing such a positive attitude with confidence is not an easy task. Having strong determination and faith that we can achieve our goal may help us surmount obstacles.

Our attitude toward suffering is an important factor in enabling us to rise above life's difficulties. The Bahá'í writings emphasize the significance of educating and raising children with an attitude of acceptance of life's hardships and an ability to face difficulties. Spiritual education can nurture in us a positive attitude and a willingness to face life's trials.[19]

Meditating on the nature and outcome of adversity helps us to discern the wisdom and benefit of difficult experiences. 'Abdu'l-Bahá explains that life ordeals are often blessings in disguise:

When the winds blow severely, rains fall fiercely, the lightning flashes, the thunder roars, the bolt descends and storms of trial become severe, grieve not; for after this storm, verily, the divine spring will arrive, the hills and fields will become verdant, the expanses of grain will joyfully wave, the earth will become covered with blossoms, the trees will be clothed with green garments and adorned with blossoms and fruits. Thus blessings become manifest in all countries. These favors are results of those storms and hurricanes. The discerning man rejoiceth at the day of trials. . . .[20]

THE WISDOM AND MYSTERY OF SUFFERING

Suffering may afflict people for many reasons. For some it may be due to their shortcomings and the nature of their behavior. For others, it may be to raise their consciousness of the true purpose of life in this world. For many, it can have an ennobling effect on their character and empower them to detach themselves from excessive material attachment and become submissive to the will of God. In the following passage, 'Abdu'l-Bahá provides some perspective on the tragic event of the *Titanic* disaster:

Within the last few days a terrible event has happened in the world, an event saddening to every heart and grieving every spirit. I refer to the Titanic disaster, in which many of our fellow human beings were drowned, a number of beautiful souls passed beyond this earthly life. Although such an event is indeed regrettable, we must realize that everything which happens is due to some wisdom and that nothing happens without a reason. . . . I am very sad indeed. But when I consider this calamity in another aspect, I am consoled by the realization that the worlds of God are infinite; that though they were deprived of this existence, they have other opportunities in the life beyond, even as Christ has said, "In my Father's house are many mansions. . . .

These human conditions may be likened to the matrix of the mother from which a child is to be born into the spacious outer world. At first the infant finds it very difficult to reconcile itself to its new existence. It cries as if not wishing to be separated from its narrow abode and imagining that life is restricted to that limited space. It is reluctant to leave its home, but nature forces it into this world. Having come into its new conditions, it finds that it has passed from darkness into a sphere of radiance; from gloomy and restricted surroundings it has been transferred to a spacious and delightful environment . . . it looks with wonder and delight upon the mountains, meadows and fields of green, the rivers and fountains, the wonderful stars; it breathes the life-quickening atmosphere; and then it praises God for its release from the confinement of its former condition and attainment to the freedom of a new realm. This analogy expresses the relation of the temporal world to the life hereafter—the transition of the soul of man from darkness and uncertainty to the light and reality of the eternal Kingdom. . . .

Furthermore, these events have deeper reasons. Their object and purpose is to teach man certain lessons. We are living in a day of reliance upon material conditions. Men imagine that the great size and strength of a ship, the perfection of machinery or the skill of a navigator will ensure safety, but these disasters sometimes take place that men may know that God is the real Protector.

Let no one imagine that these words imply that man should not be thorough and careful in his undertakings. God has endowed man with intelligence so that he may safeguard and protect himself. Therefore, he must provide and surround himself with all that scientific skill can produce . . . yet, withal, let him rely upon God and consider God as the one Keeper. If God protects, nothing can imperil man's safety, and if it be not His will to safeguard, no amount of preparation and precaution will avail.[21]

In conclusion, we need to perceive tests and adversity in a larger context: the purpose of human creation, which is to know and to worship the Creator and to advance an everlasting civilization. In such a context, life is basically a spiritual journey during which tests and suffering are unavoidable to attain perfection and the higher virtues.

10

Life Crises, Trauma, and Growth

"Be thou strong and firm. Be thou resolute and steadfast. When the tree is firmly rooted, it will bear fruit . . . The trials of God are many, but if man remains firm and steadfast, test itself is a stepping stone for the progress of humanity."

—'Abdu'l-Bahá

Traditionally, traumatic and distressing experiences have been perceived to be the cause of emotional disturbance and misfortune. Tragic and traumatic experiences can have serious emotional and psychosocial consequences, yet it is important to realize that many individuals who suffer from traumatic life events are able to bounce back with resilience and creativity.

Whatever threatens an individual's well-being, safety, or personal integrity often provokes serious fear and anxiety. The duration of a traumatic experience can cause a long and sometimes lifelong emotional disturbance, resulting in anger, guilt, insomnia, anxiety, or depression, all of which are common but not universal. Depending on personal adaptive resources, the long-term reactions of different individuals to trauma can vary.

POST-TRAUMATIC GROWTH

Tedeschi and Calhoun have conceptualized the following notion of post-traumatic growth: experiencing highly challenging life crises may result in a positive change that can manifest itself in a variety of ways. This change includes a greater appreciation of life, an increased sense of personal strength, and a change of priorities that results in a richer existential and spiritual life. Such growth after a traumatic experience interacts with life development and the acquisition of wisdom, which is an ongoing process, not a static one. However, it is to be noted that traumatic experiences should not be perceived as precursors of growth. A distinction needs to be made between resilience and growth after a life crisis. In resilience, there is an ability to continue living a purposeful life after adversity. In post-traumatic growth, however, the trauma is beyond one's ability to resist, but a transformation occurs through overcoming the crisis.[1]

The question is, can life crises or challenges serve as catalysts for growth, and if there is such a possibility, what is the mechanism or process? Is it possible that some individuals with greater capacity can bounce back while those who don't have social skills will fail? According to Tedeschi and Calhoun, "Growth, however, does not occur as a direct result of trauma. It is the individual's struggle with the new reality in the aftermath of trauma that is crucial in determining the extent to which posttraumatic growth occurs."[2] These authors use the metaphor of an earthquake in exploring post-traumatic growth. A physical earthquake or seismic event can severely shake, shatter, or even reduce to rubble a town or city. Similarly, a psychological seismic event can shock, threaten, or traumatize the confidence and cognitive function that is used to guide one's understanding and decision-making process. A psychological earthquake or trauma may challenge, contradict, or even nullify an individual's understanding and assumptions about various issues. After a natural or physical earthquake, people begin to rebuild and restructure the disaster area. After a traumatic experience, cognitive processing and restructuring occurs as well.

After a physical earthquake, the rebuilding will be designed to make the affected areas more resistant and stronger to withstand shocks in the future. Likewise, cognitive rebuilding will incorporate a more realistic durability and resistance to future crises in order to prevent a person's psyche from being shattered. This new development constitutes a phenomenon of growth.[3]

Brain plasticity and capability, as well as psychological resilience, enable a person to become a survivor and to bounce back from a traumatic experience, just as a community rebuilds after an earthquake. Spiritual insight also gives hope and purpose to the entire process of psychological reconstruction for survival. The process of transformation is not only a cognitive process—it also incorporates emotional and spiritual experiences. Together these new experiences sustain the new change in the person.

Certain types of behavioral qualities may contribute to personal growth after traumatic experiences or major life crises. These characteristics include extroversion, openness to life experience, optimism, and sociability with an available support system. But these qualities can't be generalized. In addition to the characteristics of extroversion and introversion, a deeper perspective on life's meaning and purpose, a sense of faith, and a spiritual understanding of the ultimate goals of life are prerequisites for healing from traumatic events. Indeed, some of those who made heroic personal progress after suffering a debilitating disease were not outgoing or extroverted but were rather shy or introverted.

HELEN KELLER:
A JOURNEY THROUGH LIFE WITHOUT SIGHT AND SOUND

When Helen Keller was less than two years old, she came down with a fever that left her blind, deaf, and consequently mute. Forced to live in a dark and silent world, she became increasingly conscious of her incapacity and developed into a wild and unruly child. Later on in life she wrote, "Sometimes I stood between two persons who were conversing and touched their lips. I could not understand and was vexed. I moved my lips and gesticulated frantically without results. This made me so angry at times that I kicked and screamed until I was exhausted."[4]

When she was seven years old, a teacher from the Perkins Institute for the Blind, Ann Sullivan, gradually taught her to "hear" by spelling words into her hand and to "see" by touching objects. Later Helen learned to talk and to know what others said to her by touching lips and other parts of the mouth. Thus, through perseverance and the creative approaches of her gifted teacher, she learned how to communicate with the world. She graduated from Radcliffe College at age twenty-four and spent her life helping and inspiring others with similar problems. She wrote articles, gave lectures, and raised funds for the American Foundation for the Blind. At the age of eighty, the Foundation for the Overseas Blind honored her by naming an international award after her. Her life demonstrates the power of determination to overcome extreme limitations.

SUFFERING AND HUMAN VALUES

Human values are the highest expression of a person's conviction, integrity, and character. They are the fruits of acquired and innate knowledge and personal development. To defend one's personal and spiritual values in the face of adversity is an act of faith and fulfillment. Alexander Herzen has commented, "To realize the relative validity of one's convictions and yet stand for them unflinchingly is what distinguishes a civilized man from a barbarian."[5] Viktor Frankl, a noted psychiatrist who survived the Nazi concentration camps, identifies three types of values:

- Values that are actualized by action;
- Values that are experiential and are realized through passive receiving;
- Attitudinal values that are actualized when a person is faced with something unalterable, "something imposed by destiny."

He further states that from the manner in which a person takes these things upon himself, assimilates these difficulties into his own psyche, there flows an incalculable multitude of value potentialities.[6]

An expression of human values depends not only on personal will but also on the circumstances that confront an individual wishing to make his or her values known to others. These circumstances may involve day-to-day, nonthreatening interpersonal situations or situations that challenge and undermine the individual's values and beliefs. Thus, an expression of personal values may occur in either a friendly or a life-threatening environment. Perseverance in one's religious beliefs in the face of persecution is a process that enables a person to actualize his or her spiritual values. Denying one's beliefs, however, would prevent one from actualizing them and would go against one's personal convictions.[7] Sometimes such perseverance does not occur in the face of persecution or the repression of certain beliefs or ideologies. Rather, it occurs for the promotion of a higher ideal for the betterment of humanity, such as a new world order (the future divine civilization based on the teachings of the Bahá'í Faith).

MARION JACK: A GIFTED ARTIST AND SHINING PIONEER

Marion Jack was a Canadian artist who was born into a family with six children in New Brunswick. She suffered many losses early in life. By the age of nine, three of her siblings had died. By age nineteen, she had lost both of her parents. She was ill most of her life. 'Abdu'l-Bahá, whom she visited in Acre before World War I, admired her sense of humor, joviality, and spiritual certitude. In 1931, at the age of sixty-five, she visited the

Holy Land again and was advised by Shoghi Effendi, the Guardian of the Bahá'í Faith, to travel to Sofia, Bulgaria—which she did in spite of her physical illness. Later, as World War II was beginning, she was advised by Shoghi Effendi to leave Bulgaria, but she requested to be allowed to stay. She persevered as a pioneer (one who moves to another country or region to promote the teachings of the Bahá'í Faith) in a foreign land with heroic steadfastness and sacrifice, particularly during a time of terrible war. Describing her stay there, Shoghi Effendi wrote:

> She was bombed, evacuated, she slept in some drafty, cold room in a school in the country, was often, we have reason to believe, almost hungry, and insufficiently clad after the war, due to difficulties in getting money through to her in a Soviet-dominated territory. She never mastered the language, and was without friends of her own country; and yet, she persevered, and, in spite of even the Guardian's pleas that she leave the country during the worst years of the war, remained at her post, won for herself imperishable fame, her resting-place becoming a shrine in Bulgaria, which the people of that country will increasingly honor and cherish.

Her resolute perseverance despite much deprivation and suffering won her the title of an "immortal heroine" and was "a shining example to pioneers of present and future generations" as described by Shoghi Effendi.[8]

We are surrounded and constantly influenced by the materialistic lifestyle of society. In such an environment, to lead a life of simplicity and moderation is a formidable task. Consumerism has blurred our perception of our environment, our friends and family, and even our own selves. Because of this blurred vision of ourselves, we may sometimes not recognize who we are. Being our true self requires a conviction deeply rooted in our spiritual reality. If material success and achievements become our fondest goals, and if we fail to attain these goals, we may feel as though we have totally failed in life and sink into a state of vulnerability.

Viktor Frankl stated that human existence consists of being conscious and responsible. One's responsibility is to actualize one's values. The opportunity to actualize values not only varies from time to time but also from person to person. According to Frankl, "human life . . . can be fulfilled not only in creating and enjoying, but also in suffering. Those who worship the superficial cult of success obviously will not understand such conclusions." He gives the example of a person who plunges into the water to save the life of someone who is drowning. In the end, however, both are drowned. Then he asks if such an act is less ethical because of the outcome. He concludes that lack of success in such circumstances does not signify lack of meaning.[9]

BAHÍYYIH KHÁNUM:
RESILIENCE AND CONTENTMENT AMIDST ADVERSITY

Bahíyyih Khánum, also known as the Greatest Holy Leaf, was the eldest daughter of the Prophet Founder of the Bahá'í Faith, Bahá'u'lláh. She was born in Iran into a noble family but spent almost all the days of her life in exile, captivity, and affliction, mostly in foreign lands. She achieved the highest rank of any woman in the Bahá'í dispensation and was one of the greatest sufferers the world has witnessed. In a letter written after her passing on behalf of Shoghi Effendi, her great nephew, we read, "The sufferings she bore in the pathway of God were the cruelest ones. Fortitude was the rich dress she wore, serenity and tranquil strength were her splendid robe, virtue and detachment, purity and chastity, were all her jewels, and tenderness, care and love for humankind, her beauty's bright adornings." From early childhood, she shared the sorrow and sufferings, hardships and tribulations of her father. Yet instead of protesting and being defiant, she accepted these tests and sufferings because of the profound meaning she drew from them, a meaning and a purpose that she believed would transform the oppression and social injustice of an old and decadent world order of the past into a system of peace and prosperity for the entire human race. For her, the suffering she endured was transformed into a force of change toward a new world order.[10]

She cherished the oppressed Bahá'í community of her time as the building block of a future civilization. Therefore she persevered with astonishing courage, faith, and optimism. Shoghi Effendi himself wrote, "No calamity, however intense, could obscure the brightness of her saintly face, and no agitation, no matter how severe, could disturb the composure of her gracious and dignified behavior." Serenity and fortitude in the face of ordeals was a sign of the nobility of her character and a reflection of the victory of her soul as well as her reliance on divine assistance. Yet she remained realistic and practical, actively pursuing creative solutions in day-to-day life and confronting challenges and hostile attacks with confidence. She suffered afflictions, poverty, loneliness, and exile with a spirit of acquiescence and loving patience.[11]

She wrote that all the virtues of humankind are summed up in one word: "'steadfastness,' if we but act according to its laws." Furthermore she wrote, "Steadfastness is a treasure that makes a man so rich as to have no need of the world or of anything that is therein . . . Constancy is a special joy . . ."[12]

Bahíyyih Khánum was a champion of steadfastness and resilience herself. For over eighty years she shared the suffering of her father, then her brother, and finally her great-nephew. She endured exile after exile, filled with the torment of persecution and losses, and in spite of her continued suffering, she remained resilient. The passing of her elder brother, 'Abdu'l-Bahá, while in exile had a terrible impact on her as she wrote, "Ever since that most grievous of disasters, the passing of 'Abdu'l-Bahá, this world of dust has become a cage, and a place of torment; and to the unrestrained nightingales it is only a prison, narrow and dark." She related to the sufferings of 'Abdu'l-Bahá, with whom she had shared many tribulations, and of him she wrote, "That prisoner, grievously wronged, would hide His pain, and keep His wounds from view. In the depths of calamity he would smile, and even when enduring the direst of afflictions He would comfort the hearts. Although He was hemmed about with disasters, and living at the whirlwind's core of grief, He would still proclaim the Cause of God, and protect the Holy Faith." Yet she felt comforted by the fact that these tribulations were for a great purpose, and she stated, "Nevertheless, the all-compelling will of God and His all-encompassing and irresistible purpose has desired that this dark earth should become as the Abhá Kingdom, and this heap of dust be changed until it becomes the envy of the rose gardens of Heaven."[13]

THE TRIAD OF OPPRESSION—RESILIENCE

On the basis of the above analysis, the impact of a stressor such as oppression may depend on three factors as follows:

- Intensity of the oppression;
- Personal endurance and resilience;
- Spiritual or ideological perception and attitude toward oppression (personal interpretation of the event).[14]

Based on this model, the severity of oppression (such as trauma, torment, or persecution) may not significantly disturb the subject if the person is prepared to endure for a cause and finds a meaning in it that would give purpose to his or her life. Although the severity of oppression directed toward an individual is usually beyond his or her control, resilience and a behavioral attitude are important factors within his or her power, and both resilience and attitude are influenced by spiritual or sociocultural beliefs. In this process, the attitude will strengthen the will to endure and to resist the oppression. For example, among the survivors of concentration camps, those who reportedly maintained a hopeful, positive attitude or displayed active resistance fared better in survival over those who were passive victims because the resistance activated self-esteem and contact with the outside world. Throughout the persecution of the Bahá'ís of Iran, who are members of an unrecognized religious minority in that country, the government of Iran has often tried to force the Bahá'ís to recant their faith to gain their freedom and rights. However, the majority of Bahá'ís in Iran have steadfastly refused to recant even when forced to submit to torture, imprisonment, and the threat of execution, and today they continue to demonstrate their resilience. This refusal has continued to anger the authorities, who have intensified their repression even to this day.[15]

TRANSFORMATION OF HATE INTO LOVE: A CREATIVE PROCESS

The above examples of the ability to overcome the natural tendency to return hate with hate does not happen spontaneously. The mystic transformation of hate into love is the result of a spiritual education free from prejudices. This type of education empowers a person to change. It would be very difficult, if not impossible, for one to develop such a capacity for personal transformation without the aid of spiritual insight and faith. This insight and faith can be acquired through the knowledge of and love for God.[16]

Prejudices, whether religious or political, play a powerful role in the perception and suffering of the victim in the mind of the persecutor. Under the influence of political ideology or religious fanaticism, the mind can dissociate the knowledge of pain and suffering from its real feeling and experience. When feeling is dissociated from the reality of perception, and when the conscience is no longer in contact with the mind, the behavioral consequences can be tragic. A distinguishing feature of the responses elicited by the brutal persecution of the Bahá'ís of Iran is the nonviolent and peaceful attitude of the Bahá'ís in the face of adversity. They have continually reacted with patience and tolerance to aggression and hatred.[17]

RESPONSES TO PERSECUTION

In a world rampant with hatred and persecution of various types, developing a sensible strategy for response is a personal journey. Our response can be dispassionate and logical or emotionally charged and irrational. Our reaction to a distressing event may also be affected by culture and the social climate in which we live. According to Rutter, "Resistance to stress is relative, not absolute; the bases of the resistance are both environmental and constitutional; and the degree of resistance is not a fixed quality—rather it varies over time and according to circumstances."[18] Resistance can also have a spiritual dimension, which has not yet been fully explored in modern psychology. This dimension is based on spiritual education, belief, and insight into the nature of human beings and the purpose of their creation.

Exposure to adversities as they come about in the course of life may improve our adaptability in facing life events. Indeed, on the one hand, hardship and difficult experiences of an earlier period of life may serve as a form of psychological vaccination and personal preparation that can strengthen the individual to cope better with future life experiences. On the other hand, unresolved traumatic conflicts of childhood may create a psychological climate that can complicate personal development in later life. These kinds of traumatic experiences requiring treatment should not be confused with hardship and difficulties due to, for example, socioeconomic deprivations that many have had to face at some point in life.

In addition to acquiring psychological coping mechanisms, one also needs to come to terms with the reality of stressful life events and their meaning. This is a process of making an internal adjustment to a difficult problem of an external nature. Depending on educational and cultural attitudes, coping mechanisms may vary greatly from person to person. In a life crisis of serious proportion, such as a death in the family, the following phases of mourning may take place: shock, denial, despair, recognition, and acceptance. An individual's attitude toward death and belief in life after death will have an important bearing on the ability to cope.[19]

SUFFERING, MASOCHISM, AND FANATICISM

On the subject of persecution, it is important that a distinction be made between the concepts of suffering, masochism and fanaticism. Masochism has been described as "pleasure derived from physical or psychological pain inflicted either by oneself or by others."[20] The acceptance of pain and suffering for persevering in one's belief, whether spiritual or scientific, should not be confused with masochism. For example, a scientist who makes new discoveries often faces the challenge of resistance, rejection, or opposition until his or her new thesis is proven to be true. Likewise, a person who chooses to tread the path of a new spiritual truth may have to be content with adversities for daring to be different from those who oppose his or her views. Neither the former nor the latter person intentionally seeks pain and torment for personal satisfaction in the pursuit of perfection. In a masochistic pursuit, however, the individual seeks or incites situations where pain or punishment becomes a means of gratification for certain emotional or instinctual needs.

The Bahá'í view of suffering differs from that of some other religions in that suffering is not seen as a means for personal salvation or to attain the reward of paradise. Nor is it believed that an individual is born sinful and therefore should suffer. The Bahá'í Faith teaches that human beings are essentially noble creatures, and it sees in inevitable suffering a challenge for personal growth. In the Bahá'í Faith, the human soul is believed to be unaffected by physical pain and afflictions. An example of this can be seen in the life of the persecuted Bahá'ís of Iran and early believers of other religions of the world. In spite of every conceivable type of torture and inhuman adversity, they remained calm and content, reflecting many noble attributes. Indeed, undergoing suffering may have transformed their lower and material qualities into higher and spiritual attributes.[21]

11

Spiritual Dimensions
of Suffering and Creativity

"There is no doubt that the tests are severe. The more a soul resists and shows firmness and steadfastness, the greater will be his progress, and he shall soar to the sublimest heights of the Kingdom."

—*'Abdu'l-Bahá*

In the Bahá'í writings, sufferings and privations are considered blessings in disguise, and through them "our inner spiritual forces become stimulated, purified and ennobled." Trials and tribulations are sometimes preordained, and there is a great wisdom in these occurrences, as stated by Shoghi Effendi: "Whatsoever comes to pass in the Cause of God, however disquieting in its immediate effects, is fraught with infinite Wisdom and tends ultimately to promote its interests in the world." Submission to the will of God is an essential attitude of Bahá'ís who are faced with adversities beyond their control. In materialistic societies, self-centeredness and material attachment become an impediment to one's submission to the greater will, and therefore discontent is prevalent. In such an environment, personal contentment is often sought through material possessions and success rather than through spiritual fulfillment. In the Seven Valleys, Bahá'u'lláh describes the traveler of the Valley of Knowledge with these words: "He in this station is content with the decree of God, and seeth war as peace, and findeth in death the secrets of everlasting life. With inward and outward eyes he witnesseth the mysteries of resurrection in the realms of creation and the souls of men, and with a pure heart apprehendeth the divine wisdom in the endless Manifestations of God. In the ocean he findeth a drop, in a drop he beholdeth the secrets of the sea."[1] Viewing suffering as a blessing in disguise should be understood in light of the fact that there is often a hidden and profound wisdom in the occurrence of a life crisis or ordeal, the meaning of which is beyond our understanding.

Therefore, the above statement should not be taken as a longing to glorify or seek out suffering for the sake of entitlement or heroism. Instead, it underlines the need to be patient and content with the will of God at a time when efforts to solve a crisis fail. Bahá'u'lláh's words in the Seven Valleys are deeply mystic and endowed with profound meaning, requiring much reflection in order to comprehend them.

HEROISM AND RESILIENCE WITH FAITH

As a testimony to the degree of faith and certitude displayed by Bahá'ís in facing life-threatening crises, the following example demonstrates the undaunted conviction of a number of persecuted Bahá'ís of Iran who were tortured and killed because of their religion. The example reflects the magnitude of the spiritual dimension of human responses to persecution. The eyewitness account, given by a Bahá'í prisoner, is evidence of the brutal attempts of fanatical tormentors to break the resistance of a fellow inmate in Iran:

They tried to force her to recant, and the guards whipped her with wire cables. Because she was a woman they had covered her back with a cotton chador, because it would have been immodest for them to see her bare back. The wires had torn her back to shreds, so that you could see the bone, but they had also torn the chador to shreds and the pieces of rag had been whipped into the raw flesh on her back. They whipped her until she was unconscious and threw her in the cell. Then another group of guards came in and said they needed Yaldai for her trial. We all said she couldn't be tried because she was unconscious. They just grabbed her by the arms, with her feet trailing on the floor. She told us that when they were beating her they said they could stop if she would go on radio and television to publicly deny her faith and to say that the Bahá'ís spied for Israel. She was in the cell for 55 days without medical attention. Finally she was taken away and hanged with nine other women who had also refused to recant.[2]

She was one of ten Bahá'í women who were imprisoned, tortured, and eventually killed in the city of Shiraz. Their so-called crime was their allegiance to the Bahá'í Faith. Their decision to accept suffering was based on their belief in the truth of the mission of Bahá'u'lláh and His teachings, which gave meaning to their lives and to their sacrifice. This sacrifice gave meaning to their actions, according to Viktor Frankl, who said, "Suffering ceases to be suffering in some way at the moment it finds a meaning such as the meaning of sacrifice."[3]

In the history of humanity countless men and women have paid a heavy price for defending their beliefs. To them, recanting was against their moral principles and was a denial of a most cherished goal of their lives. As Albert Einstein once stated, "Great spirits have always encountered violent opposition from mediocre minds."[4]

PSYCHOLOGICAL AND SPIRITUAL RESPONSES TO STRESS

Table 1 below shows a comparison of stress responses influenced by spiritual insight as compared to responses due to psychological defenses. The strength of a spiritual response depends largely on an individual's reliance on faith and his or her capacity to reflect this reliance in deeds. Therefore, just as individuals are different, the strength of their spiritual responses may be different as well. Indeed, some fail or falter when subjected to atrocities and are unable to respond with the necessary fortitude to remain optimistic during hardship.[5]

TABLE 1*

Some Responses to Severe Social Stressors

Psychological Responses	Spiritual Responses
Denial or perplexity	Acknowledgment and forbearance
Amnesia or selective attention	Perceptivity and full attention
Fear	Courage
Avoidance and withdrawl	Affiliation and acceptance
Counterbehavior, e.g., fight or flight	Expression of love and tolerance
Disillusionment and discontent	Certitude and contentment
Dependence solely on self	Submission to the Will of God
Coping through reason	Reaching beyond reason to faith

* Original version published in Ghadirian, "Human responses to life stress and suffering," 60.

An individual's attitude toward death and his or her belief in life after death will have an important bearing on his or her ability to cope with hardship. Therefore, adaptational responses are not elicited universally in an identical fashion, and there are considerable variations, depending on individual belief, character, and life experience. Tolerance and magnanimity have been observed among the early believers of each religion and even among certain pioneers of science who defied opposition with peaceful tolerance and raised questions concerning the validity of the stress response theory in the face of life crises. One explanation could be that when the life threat, whether psychological or physical, can be explained and made sense of in the light of scientific or spiritual conviction, this insight will arouse considerable courage, which will, in turn, abate the fear and anxiety created by the threat. Moreover, faith itself is a potent force in which human beings find their ultimate fulfillment. With true faith, one sees in an inevitable death a fulfillment of one's spiritual convictions. Thus faith gives new meaning to suffering, and it can transform fear into joy and despair into hope. For example, the heroic life of the martyrs of the Bahá'í Faith, their determination and perseverance for their cause in spite of torture and torments inflicted upon them, testify to the strength of their faith and the loftiness of their beliefs in a cause for which they gave their most precious possession: life itself. This is a triumph of the soul in the pursuit of a higher ideal or truth for which contemporary science is at a loss to find an answer.[6]

The history of religions shows that human tolerance to suffering goes far beyond the psychological formulation of defenses and stress adaptation. In such cases, suffering is perceived neither as a destructive force of despair and agony nor as a grievous blow to human defenses. Rather, it is welcomed with faith and contentment. This does not imply that victims of religious persecution are always entirely free from pain and sorrow; instead, it suggests that their spiritual conviction and faith have changed their perception and attitude toward suffering and have empowered them to gain greater tolerance. No one knows with scientific certainty at present how a profound spiritual conviction can raise the physiological threshold of pain and suffering, since neither spirituality nor suffering is an experience that can be measured and quantified biochemically or physiologically.

LEARNING FROM ADVERSITY

Although severe life stressors and adversities may increase the risk of emotional disturbances—such as depression in the face of personal losses—usually most people do not succumb to these diseases. Most of those who suffer personal losses do not necessarily become clinically depressed and incapacitated, although they are affected by these losses. According to Rutter, "Resistance to stress is relative, not absolute; the bases of the resistance are both environmental and constitutional; and the degree of resistance is not a fixed quality—rather it varies over time and according to circumstances." Resistance can also have a spiritual dimension, which has not yet been fully explored in modern psychology. This dimension is based on spiritual education, belief, and insight into the nature of human beings and the purpose of their creation.[7]

Life crises generate intense fear and distress, which are defense responses. But crises also challenge our belief in having control over our destiny. Suppression or denial of distrustful emotions are not solutions. It is important to empathize with the suffering individual and help him or her to process the distress and draw meaning from the painful events. Distressful events can serve as a catalyst for change and transformation, and not all who are struck by life shattering experiences become incapacitated with post-traumatic stress disorder (PTSD). Time, meditation, and a supportive environment can also increase adaptability and help the person to come to terms with a new reality. Through this new insight, people can reorganize their life and priorities. Sometimes ego and narcissistic attachment to self can become obstacles in the road to recovery. Campbell has written, "When you take the self out of the picture, sometimes the world emerges as more powerful, as wondrous." Negative life events have the ability "to shake up the status quo" in one's life and open the door for change.[8]

Exposure to adversity in the course of life may improve our adaptability in facing life events. Indeed, on the one hand, hardship and difficult experiences of an earlier period of life may serve as a form of psychological vaccination and personal preparation that strengthen the individual to cope better in the future. On the other hand, unresolved traumatic childhood conflicts may create a psychological climate that can complicate personal development in later life. Traumatic experiences such as these that require treatment should not be confused with day-to-day hardships and difficulties and their associated challenges.[9]

Recent research on survivors of torture shows that repeated exposure to stress may immunize some against subsequent traumatic experiences. Social and emotional support by family and friends plays an important role in protecting against or overcoming traumatic experiences.[10] Researchers have debated the impact of stress on individuals and the development of PTSD. While some believe that generally a person will develop a form of neurosis if the stress is strong enough, others maintain that a traumatic experience is not sufficient to cause PTSD in every person exposed to it. (In this context, *stress* refers to a distressing life event that is beyond the range of usual human experience. It is also to be noted that individual vulnerability and genetic predisposition to stress vary from person to person.) These divergent views show the complex and multidimensional nature of human vulnerability and resilience to stressful events.[11]

Beyond the scientific exploration of traumatic experiences and human resilience, we should be conscious of the spiritual forces and potential (free from fanaticism) that would strengthen our endurance and give a new meaning to life in the face of adversity. In our struggle to be creative amidst life crises, we need to keep a balance between our mind and our soul. Indeed, as 'Abdu'l-Bahá has pointed out, "Religion and Science are inter-twined with each other and cannot be separated. These two are wings with which humanity must fly."[12]

CONCLUSION

To experience life crises and suffering, whether individually or collectively as part of a group, carries a meaning, the understanding of which is important for personal and collective growth and progress. Traditionally we have associated adversity and suffering with negative and destructive connotations. This is natural, as we can't deny the pain of loss, tyranny, or other human tragedies. But the ability to rise above all limitations and to create a condition that is conducive to transforming the darkness of suffering into the bright light of hope and meaningfulness is a creative achievement.

Conclusion

The interrelationship between suffering and creativity is a vast and fascinating area to explore, and yet it is fraught with many challenges. To transform life crises and adversities into a process of growth and creative outcome is a formidable task, but it can also be looked at as an art form. To determine why some people succeed while others fail or are crushed by life crisis calls for a broader perspective not only of the extent and intensity of life struggles and calamities but also a better understanding of human nature and the biological, psychological, social, and spiritual aspects of individual capacity. Moreover, the evolution of human potential to overcome adversity deals largely with subjective experiences that are far removed from a materialistic evidence-based approach of measuring outcomes and applying statistical methodology.

To experience life crises, whether in the form of physical violence or emotional affliction, carries meaning that affects an individual's attitude in dealing with future crises. Traditionally we have associated adversity and suffering with negative and destructive connotations. Culture and childhood education often reinforce such impressions, the results of which are fear and anxiety. This kind of impression of the dark side of suffering is partly understandable; as human beings we are vulnerable and can't avoid the pain and grief of facing loss or tragedy. But our education and socio-cultural beliefs underestimate human biological and psychological resilience and our potential to confront and possibly conquer many trials and tribulations. To sustain such an empowering vision and insight, a shift of consciousness needs to take place in our mindset to acknowledge possible positive and creative potential amidst adversity. Such an acknowledgment by itself can motivate us to look beyond the dark cloud of doom and gloom to search for the light of hope and alternative responses. The ability to rise above all limitations and reach a condition that will be conducive to transforming the darkness of suffering into the bright light of hope and meaningfulness is a creative triumph. Such an achievement, however, will not be pain-free or without difficulties. Transformation comes with its own pain, but it is a growing pain unlike the angst of peril.

Suffering is a process, and so is creativity. A process implies a journey; it is not so much about reaching a destination as about what is involved in getting there. In this journey, the more a traveler is consciously aware of the purpose and meaning of the journey and its destination, the more he or she will be prepared to encounter adversity with creative planning. In today's world, from the threat of nuclear disaster to massive hurricanes, and from the danger of terrorism to unforeseeable tsunamis, humanity—though at the height of scientific achievement—is gripped by fear and anguish and is unaware of the source or meaning of these catastrophic developments. According to Bahá'í belief, the most important creative force behind this global threat is a process of the reconstruction of society, based on a new world order that will guide humanity and usher in a more just and unified society. As long as the world community is unable or unwilling to recognize the meaning and purpose of this force, it will continue to live with fear and trepidation.

In this book the focus of overcoming life struggles has been mainly on the individual level. Those who rise to victory over their mental or physical challenges can serve as an inspiration not only to their family and friends, but also to society. As 'Abdu'l-Bahá has stated, "the honor and distinction of the individual consists in this, that he among all the world's multitudes should become a source of social good. Is any larger bounty conceivable than this, that an individual, looking within himself, should find that by the confirming grace of God he has become the cause of peace and well-being, of happiness and advantage to his fellow men?"[1] Individuals who struggle to become "the cause of peace and well-being" of others are, in a sense, on a creative path for social good and justice.

In explaining human suffering and adversity, this analysis has been based on the notion that people are essentially spiritual beings whose physical frame provides them with the necessary instrument to fulfill their potential during this earthly life. The purpose of human creation is to know and to worship God, and to contribute to the advancement of social justice and the unity of humankind. This recognition of the spiritual nature of human beings should not be viewed as the antithesis of science and technology, which are also extremely important and are extolled in the Bahá'í writings.

Indeed, the Bahá'í writings envisage a world in which society will have the capacity to "extend the range of human and technical development, to the increase of the productivity of mankind, to the extermination of disease, to the extension of scientific research, to the raising of the standard of physical health, to the sharpening and refinement of the human brain . . . to the prolongation of human life, and to the furtherance of any other agency that can stimulate the intellectual, the moral, and spiritual life of the entire human race."[2]

With such a viewpoint we can expand our vision of personal growth and creativity to activities beyond the creation of magnificent works of art. For example, developing an imaginative educational program for children and youth who will acquire moral virtues and capabilities for the betterment of society is an act of creativity. Such an endeavor can be even more praiseworthy if it is extended to those who have a creative interest but who are deprived as a result of a disability or other life struggles. In the Bahá'í Faith, work performed in a spirit of service is elevated to the station of worship.[3] This reflects the spiritual aspect of engagement in vocational and other productive activities.

In their research, Pargament et al. pointed out that there are three potentially critical "growth-related" spiritual ingredients in coping with life crises: 1) Spirituality may provide an important source of support and empowerment for people in distress, 2) Spirituality may play a critical role in the process of giving meaning to stressful situations, and 3) Spirituality may foster "life-changing transformation of goals and priorities" in response to serious stressors. It is also possible that some people may experience a decline in their religious belief in the aftermath of a critical trauma because they feel disappointed that their expectations were not met. This has been reported by some Holocaust survivors. Therefore responses may be different. At the time of crisis some people may perceive life trials as punishment while others may see them as blessings in disguise. Seeing life as a workshop where our learning takes place can have an empowering effect, provided that we are well equipped with coping skills and mindfulness. Being prepared will help us to rethink and prioritize our goals in life.[4]

What has been generally underestimated in literature on suffering is the power of imagination and meditation in coping with crises. Such resources are rich, but experiences with them are mostly subjective, and it is impossible to measure them in conventional scientific ways. In an environment where we try to analyze and understand everything intellectually, we may overlook the powerful effect of imagination on creativity. No less of a scientist than Albert Einstein stated, "Imagination is more important than knowledge."[5]

A significant part of this book is focused on the role of emotion and mood disorders in creativity. Many of the anecdotes are about the life and creative work of famous and accomplished artists, musicians, writers, poets, and politicians who experienced emotional turmoil or neurological and brain disorders. The main reason for the wealth of material on these well-known individuals is simply that because of their status in society, their lives, illnesses, and achievements are more thoroughly documented than those of lesser-known individuals who have struggled with similar afflictions and responded creatively. But it is important to recognize that creativity is very widespread and is not exclusive to famous individuals. As research in the field expands, there will be more studies on individuals from all walks of life and their creative responses to life crises. What is very exciting is the emergence of studies on certain mental or neurological disabilities whose victims as recently as thirty to forty years ago were considered to be completely incapacitated and doomed to spend their lives in a chronic-care institution. Now there are glimpses of hope that some of these individuals are gifted with astonishing creative ability.

The theory of a possible interrelationship between suffering and creativity is supported by research literature with special reference to studies conducted on those with a history of bipolar or other mood disorders. Likewise, more recent scientific findings in children and adults with Asperger's syndrome show encouraging signs of intellectual capability and resourcefulness despite painful social withdrawal and inhibition. Science is increasingly unraveling the link between Asperger's syndrome and creativity and is dispelling past misconceptions about the nature of this disease.

Likewise, new research in the development of frontotemporal dementia is opening a new horizon rarely observed before. Researchers have noted that some patients, in spite of their disabilities in speech, comprehension and memory, manifested specific artistic talents such as the ability to paint—abilities they had either never demonstrated before or had lost and rediscovered during the illness. Although the mechanism of such creative development and its relationship with the illness remain unclear, there are possible psychoneurological pathways that need to be explored in order to explain this phenomenon. Any progress in this domain will not only increase our understanding about the positive aspects of FTD but also may prove to be a ground-breaking discovery in finding a new treatment for it.

In any kind of suffering and ordeal, we need to adapt a positive attitude toward life and accept the reality of life struggles. Setting aside natural disasters and those technological catastrophes that are beyond our control, the degree of our attachment to a materialistic way of life can be a source of bitter struggle and ordeals. To remedy this, we need to become more creative by expanding our understanding of the purpose of our creation and embracing life with contentment and spiritual insight. With such an attitude, suffering will not be feared but rather accepted, and its deeper meaning reflected upon to achieve personal growth and transformation.

As the Universal House of Justice has written, "Man's physical existence on this earth is a period during which the moral exercise of his free will is tried and tested in order to prepare his soul for the other worlds of God, and we must welcome affliction and tribulations as opportunities for improvement in our eternal selves."[6]

Notes

Introduction
1. *Encyclopedia of Religion,* 1987, 99–101.

1 / Understanding Suffering
The epigraph is from Viktor Frankl, *Man's Search for Meaning,* 179.

1. Eliade, *Encyclopedia of Religion,* 14.99–101; Selye, Stress Without Distress, 83.

2. Eric Cassell, "The Nature of Suffering and the Goals of Medicine," 639–45.

3. 'Abdu'l-Bahá, *Paris Talks,* 35.3.

4. Ernest J. Simmons, Introduction to Dostoyevsky, *Crime and Punishment,* https://www.ecampus.com/book/9780679601005.

5. Eric Cassell, "The Relief of Suffering," 522–23.

6. Ibid.

7. H. G. Koenig et al., *Handbook of Religion and Health,* 347.

8. E. Warner, "The role of belief in healing," 1108.

9. Frankl, *Man's Search for Meaning,* 178–79.

10. Frankl, quoted in Berger, "Palliative Care in Long-Term-Care Facilities," 1570–71; Shoghi Effendi, *Unfolding Destiny,* 434.

11. W. Breitbart and K. Heller, "Reframing hope," 979–88.

12. B. M. Mount and others, "Spirituality and health," 303–8.

2 / Dimensions in Creativity
The epigraph is from Krieger, Richard Alan, *Civilization's Quotations,* 285.

1. "Definition of Creativity," http://members.optusne com:au/~char-les57/creative/Basics/definition.htm.

2. Crutch et al., "Some workmen," 2129; Fitzgerald and O'Brien, *Genius Genes,* 4; Richards and Kinney, "Mood Swings and Creativity," 202–17.

3. Richards and Kinney, "Mood Swings and Creativity," 202–17.

4. Maureen Neihart, "Creativity, the Arts and Madness," 47–50.

5. Tryk, "Assessment in the study of creativity," in *Advances in Psychological Assessments.*

6. Brenner, "Creativity and psychodynamics," 514.

7. Ibid.

8. Neihart, 47–50.

9. Richards and Kinney, "Mood Swings and Creativity," 202–17.

10. Flach, "Disorders of the Pathways," 158.

11. Helwig, "Physician-poet intrigued by the psychopathology of creative minds," 650–53.

12. 'Abdu'l-Bahá, *Some Answered Questions,* pp. 210–11; Cameron, "A proposed model of imagination and creativity," 33–36.

13. Cameron, "A proposed model of imagination and creativity," 33–36.

14. Ibid.

15. 'Abdu'l-Bahá, *Paris Talks,* 31.3, 31.6.

16. Ibid., 31.8.

17. 'Abdu'l-Bahá, *Some Answered Questions,* 210–11.

18. Ibid., 239–40.

19. Shoghi Effendi, quoted in Helen Hornby, *Lights of Guidance,* no. 385.

20. 'Abdu'l-Bahá, Tablet to August Forel, in *The Bahá'í World,* 15:37–43.

21. Springer, S. P. and G. Deutsch, *Left Brain, Right Brain,* 320–22.

22. Ibid.

23. Cassell, "The Nature of Suffering and the Goals of Medicine,"639–45.

24. 'Abdu'l-Bahá, *Some Answered Questions,* 235.

25. Bahá'u'lláh, *Gleanings,* 148.1.

3 / Resilience as a Creative Response to Suffering

The epigraph is quoted from http://www.quotationspage.com/quote/30186.html.

1. Suniya S. Luthar et al., cited in Kim-Cohen et al., "Genetic and environmental processes," 651–58; Coutu, Diane, "How Resilience Works," 48.

2. Ghadirian, "Psychological and Spiritual Dimensions of Persecution and Suffering," 13–14.

3. Lepore, S. J. and Revenson, T. A., "Resilience and posttraumatic growth," in Calhoun, L. G. and R. G. Tedeschi, *Handbook of Posttraumatic Growth,* 25.

4. Ibid., 30.

5. Calhoun, L. G. and R. G. Tedeschi, 3–23, 11.

6. Çambel, A. B., *Applied Chaos Theory,* 4.

7. Ibid., 13, 15; Henry Adams, cited in ibid., 15; Bahá'u'lláh, *Gleanings,* 70.1.

8. Grae's blog, www.imho.com/grae/chaos/chaos.html; Stewart, *Does God play dice?*, 141.

9. Zausner, "When walls become doorways," 21–28.

10. Viktor Frankl, *The Doctor and the Soul*, 81–82.

11. Ibid., 32, 85.

12. 'Abdu'l-Bahá, quoted in Esslemont, *Bahá'u'lláh and the New Era*, 67.

13. Erich Fromm, *To Have or To Be?*, 116–17; 'Abdu'l-Bahá, in *The Divine Art of Living*, 28.

14. 'Abdu'l-Bahá, *Some Answered Questions*, 157; 'Abdu'l-Bahá, quoted in Yazdani, "La dimension spirituelle des relations mere-enfant," 77; 'Abdu'l-Bahá, *Secret of Divine Civilization*, 23–24.

4 / Dimensions of Resilience and Environmental Factors

The epigraph is from Bahá'u'lláh, The Hidden Words, Arabic no. 51.

1. McGowan, "The hidden side of happiness," 70.

2. Rutter, "Resilience in the Face of Adversity," 598.

3. Ibid.

4. Segal and Weinfeld, "Do children cope better than adults," 69.

5. Ibid., 73.

6. Ibid., 75.

7. Moskavitz, "Longitudinal follow-up of child survivors of the Holocaust," 401–7; Segal and Weinfeld, "Do children cope better than adults," 75–76.

8. Segal and Weinfeld, "Do children cope better than adults," 70.

9. Siebert, *The Resiliency Advantage*, 115.

10. Caplan, G., "Mastery of stress," 413–20.

11. Rees, "Stress, distress, and disease," 3.

12. Dupont, *Selfish Brain*, 107.

13. Fettes, "Migraine Linked to Low Endorphins," 38.

14. Selye, *Stress Without Distress*, 14–16.

15. Cherry, "On the real benefits of eustress," 60–70.

16. Allen, *Coping with Trauma*, 14–15.

17. Ibid., 6.

18. Ghadirian, "Profile of stress-prone individuals," 673–79.

19. Targ, "Research methodology for studies of prayer and distant healing," 29–41.

20. 'Abdu'l-Bahá, quoted in Bahá'u'lláh and 'Abdu'l-Bahá, *The Reality of Man*, 42–43.

21. 'Abdu'l-Bahá, *Some Answered Questions*, 200; 'Abdu'l-Bahá, *'Abdu'l-Bahá in London*, 121.

22. 'Abdu'l-Bahá, quoted by May Maxwell, *An Early Pilgrimage*, p. 40.

23. Faizi, G., *Stories about 'Abdu'l-Bahá*, 11–12.

24. Helen Keller, quoted at http://www.quotationspage.com/quote/30186. html.

25. Leicester, "Cancer survivor," A1 and A4.

26. Siebert, *The Resiliency Advantage*, 32–33.

27. Ibid.

28. Burns, *Feeling Good*, 40–41.

29. Siebert, 32–33.

30. Arehart-Treichel, "Several factors critical in ability to handle crises," 12.

31. AA Prayer quoted in Kubler-Ross, *Death—the Final Stage of Growth*, xviii.

32. Arehart-Treichel, 12.

33. Long and Nielson, *Psychology Today*, 75.

34. Khan, *Prophet's Daughter*, 242–46.

35. Maddi, "Hardiness training at Illinois Bell Telephone," http://www. psychologymatters.org/hardiness.html.

36. Ibid.

37. Cousins, *Anatomy of an Illness*, 18.

38. Ibid., 27–48.

39. Ibid., 39–40.

40. Ibid.

41. APA Online, *Psychology Matters*, http://www.psychologymatters.org/ hardiness.html.

42. 'Abdu'l-Bahá, *Selections from the Writings of 'Abdu'l-Bahá*, no. 102.3; 'Abdu'l-Bahá, quoted in New Zealand Bahá'í News, Sept / Oct. 2000, 1; 'Abdu'l-Bahá, *Selections*, no. 100.2.

43. Universal House of Justice, "Message to the Bahá'ís of the World, Riḍván 157."

44. Kim-Cohen et al., 652.

45. Ibid., 661, 662–63.

46. Khavari, *Spiritual Intelligence*, 130.

47. Ibid, 137.

48. Bahá'u'lláh, The Hidden Words, Persian no. 51.

49. Capistrano School, http://www.empire.k12.ca.us/capistrano/Mike/capmusic/classical/beethoven/beethove.htm.

50. Ibid.

51. Jamer, "An incurable affliction," http://groups.msn.com. SARCOIDOSISDISEASE/general.msnw?action=get_message&mview=0&ID_Message=302&LastModified=4675526464833837699.

52. Elizabeth Gresner, http://w3.rz-berlin.mpg.de/cmp/beethoven_sym7.html.

53. Pettigrew, "I believe in miracles," 52.

54. Ibid.

55. Ibid., 220.

56. 'Abdu'l-Bahá, Star of the West, 14:41.

57. Goethe, cited in Lipowski, "Psychiatry: Mindless or Brainless," 249.

58. Bahá'u'lláh, The Bahá'í Revelation, 171; Ghadirian, "Intergenerational Responses," 530.

59. Ghadirian, "Intergenerational Responses," 524.

5 / Creativity, the Mind, and Mood

The epigraph is from 'Abdu'l-Bahá, Paris Talks, no. 57.1.

1. Written on behalf of Shoghi Effendi, Arohanui, 89; Milton, Paradise Lost.

2. Post, "Creativity and Psychopathology," 22–34, 24.

3. American News, 13.

4. Neihart, 47–50.

5. Jamison, "Manic-Depressive Illness, Genes and Creativity," 115.

6. Ibid., 62–67; Jamison, "Mood disorders," 116.

7. Jamison, "Manic-Depressive Illness, Genes and Creativity," 116.

8. Jamison, Touched with Fire, 74–75.

9. H. and K. Akiskal, "Reassessing the prevalence of bipolar disorders," 29s–36s.

10. Rothenberg, "Bipolar illness, creativity, and treatment," 133–34.

11. Schumann, quoted in Jamison, Touched with Fire, 202, 203.

12. Ibid., 203–4.

13. Goodwin and Jamison, "Manic Depressive Illness and Creativity," 345; Poe, quoted in Jamison, Touched with Fire, 192–93.

14. Flach, "Disorders of the Pathways involved in the Creative Process," 158; Jamison, "Manic Depressive Illness and Creativity," p. 66.

15. Richards and Kinney, "Mood Swings and Creativity," 202.

16. Jamison, "Manic Depressive Illness and Creativity," 66.

17. Tchaikovsky, quoted in Goodwin and Jamison, "Manic Depressive Illness and Creativity," 332.

18. Neihart, "Creativity, the Arts and Madness," 47–50.

19. Goodwin and Jamison, "Manic Depressive Illness and Creativity," 363.

20. Ibid.

21. Arehart-Treichel, "Tchaikovsky turns demons into works of beauty," 36–37.

22. Kogan, quoted in ibid., 36, 37.

23. American Psychiatric Association, *Diagnostic and Statistical Manual of Mental Disorders*, 206–7.

24. Goodwin and Jamison, "Manic Depressive Illness and Creativity," 335, 237–38.

25. Berryman, quoted in ibid., 337–38.

26. Goodwin and Jamison, "Manic Depressive Illness and Creativity," 343.

27. Ibid., 344.

28. Ibid., 345.

29. Samuel Coleridge, quoted in ibid.

30. Leonard and Virginia Woolf, quoted in Goodwin and Jamison, "Manic Depressive Illness and Creativity," 347.

31. Andreason, "Creativity and Mental Illness," 1288–92.

32. Goodwin and Jamison, "Manic Depressive Illness and Creativity," 349–50.

33. Ibid., 350.

34. Benjamin Rush, quoted in ibid., 333.

35. Richard and Kinney, "Mood Swings and Creativity," 205–8.

36. Goodwin and Jamison, "Manic Depressive Illness and Creativity," 332; Jamison, *Touched with Fire*, 240.

37. Jamison, *Touched with Fire*, 241.

38. Eisenman, "Creativity, preference for complexity and physical and mental illness," 231–36.

39. Shriqui, "Schizophrenia and the Heart of Creation," 12.

40. Ibid.

6 / Creativity and Mental Illness in Accomplished Individuals

The epigraph is from Goodwin and Jamison, "Manic Depressive Illness and Creativity," 333.

1. Richards and Kinney, "Mood Swings and Creativity," 205–8; Williams, "Abstract," R3–R4.

2. Williams, "Abstract," R3–R4.

3. Jamison, *Touched with Fire*, 102–3.

4. Storr, "Solitude," 3–4.

5. Ibid., 104; Bahá'u'lláh, *The Seven Valleys and The Four Valleys*, 8.

6. Richards et al., "Creativity in manic-depressives," 281–88.

7. Rosenthal, *Seasons of the Mind*, 202.

8. Simeonova et al., "Creativity in familial bipolar disorder," 623–31.

9. Frosch, "Moods, Madness, and Music," 316–22, 321.

10. Farnsworth, quoted in Frosch, 321.

11. R. B. Cattell, H. J. Butcher, and L. Hudson, cited in Flach, "Disorders of the Pathways involved in the Creative Process," 159.

12. Donald Goodwin, quoted in Schukit, "Creativity," 1.

13. Rosenthal, *Seasons of the Mind*, 198.

14. Carota et al., *Understanding Van Gogh's Night*, 121–31.

15. Ibid., 129.

16. Ibid., 128.

17. Goodwin and Jamison, "Manic Depressive Illness and Creativity," 358.

18. Ibid., 359.

19. Starr, cited in ibid.; Lord Moran, cited in ibid.

7 / Neurological Disability and Creativity

The epigraph is from Aristotle, cited in Goodwin and Jamison, "Manic Depressive Illness and Creativity," 333.

1. Wolfe, "Shutting down Alzheimer's," 73.

2. Crutch et al., "Some workmen can blame their tools," 2129–33.

3. Miller et al., "Enhanced artistic creativity and temporal lobe degeneration," 1744–55.

4. Ibid., 978–82.

5. Ibid.

6. Ibid.

7. Jeffrey, "How some declining dementia patients gain creative abilities," 46.

8. Miller, cited in ibid., 46.

9. Mell et al., "Art and the Brain," 1707–10.

10. Ibid.

11. Miller et al., "Functional correlates of musical and visual ability in frontotemporal dementia," 458–63.

12. Ibid., 459.

13. Ibid., 461–62.

14. Please see http://www.stephenhawking.com.

15. Rumi, quoted in Hojat, *Empathy in Patient Care*, 17.

16. Jennings, *Locked In Locked Out*, 4–8.

17. Ibid., 2–3.

18. Ibid., 10–19, 20.

19. Ibid., 22–23.

20. Ibid., 192–93.

21. Ibid., 200.

22. Cardwell, "Voyer's voyage," 29.

23. Ibid.

24. Mario Beauregard and Denyse O'Leary, *The Spiritual Brain*, 66.

25. Rossetti and Bogousslavsky, "Dostoevsky and Epilepsy," 65–75; Dostoevsky, quoted in Frankl, *Man's Search for Meaning*, 105.

26. Rossetti and Bogousslavsky, "Dostoevsky and Epilepsy," 66–70.

27. Ibid., 72–73.

28. Nash, "Going the Distance," 72.

29. Kluger, "He Never Gave Up," 53.

30. Nash, "Going the Distance," 72.

31. Christopher Reeve, quoted in ibid., 66–73.

32. Treffert and Wallace, "Islands of Genius," 78.

33. Ibid., 78–80.

34. Ibid.

35. Ibid.

36. Campbell and Shay, "Pervasive Development Disorders," 22–27.

37. Ibid., 2291, 2271–91.

38. Fitzgerald, *Autism and Creativity*; fitzgerald and O'Brien, *Genius Genes*.

39. Fitzgerald and O'Brien, *Genius Genes*, 5.

40. Ibid., 6–7.

41. Levitin et al., "Some find silver lining in hurricane clouds," p. 223

42. Ibid., 227–28.

43. Ibid., 226.

8 / Vulnerability versus Capability

The epigraph is from Bahá'u'lláh, The Hidden Words, Arabic no. 14.

1. R. S. Lazarus and S. Folman, *Stress, Appraisal, and Coping*, 77.

2. Breheny, *After the Darkest Hour*, 169.

3. Ibid., 168; Bahá'u'lláh, The Hidden Words, Arabic no. 13.

4. 'Abdu'l-Bahá, *Promulgation of Universal Peace*, 263–64.

5. Druss and Marcus, "Use of psychotropic medications before and after Sept. 11, 2001," 1377–83.

6. Levin, "Some find silver lining in hurricane clouds," 10.

7. Ibid.; Allen, *Coping with Trauma*, 17.

8. Levin, "Some find silver lining in hurricane clouds," 10.

9. Akinola and Mendes, "The dark side of creativity," 1677–86.

10. Ibid.

11. Kasi, "Creativity and Depression."

12. DuPont, Robert, *Selfish Brain*, 104; please see www.teachhealth.com/chemmess.html, 4–5.

13. Ibid., 6–7.

14. "Endorphin collection website," http://micro.magnet.fsu.edu/micro/gallery/endorphin/endorphins.html.

15. Ibid.

16. Ibid.

17. Melzak, cited in Koenig, *Handbook of Religion and Health*, 348.

18. Ibid.

19. Kiecolt-Glaser et al., "Hostile Marital Interactions," 1377–84.

20. Arehart-Treichel, "Several factors critical in ability to handle crises," 22.

21. Ibid.; Frankl, *Man's Search for Meaning*, 174.

22. Jamison, "Mood disorders," 125–34.

23. Ibid., 127.

24. Ibid., 130, 132.

25. Rosenthal, *Seasons of the Mind*, 198–99.

26. 'Abdu'l-Bahá, *Secret of Divine Civilization*, 2–3.

27. Lample, *Creating a New Mind*, 4.

28. Beil, "Using Stress to Heal," A21.

29. Ibid.

9 / Suffering, Change, and Transformation

The epigraph is from 'Abdu'l-Bahá, *Selections from the Writings of 'Abdu'l-Bahá*, no. 210.3.

1. Please see http://www.thebigview.com/buddhism/index.html.

2. 'Abdu'l-Bahá, quoted in *The Divine Art of Living*, 28.

3. Please see http://www.thebigview.com/buddhism/index.html.

4. Please see http://www.thebigview.com/buddhism/fourtruths.html#truth4.

5. Koenig et al., 349.

6. Ibid., 350.

7. 'Abdu'l-Bahá, *Paris Talks*, nos. 14.9, 57.1.

8. Ibid., no. 26.7.

9. 'Abdu'l-Bahá, *Promulgation of Universal Peace*, 451.

10. Breheny, *After the Darkest Hour*, 42.

11. Letter on behalf of the Universal House of Justice to an individual, June 23, 2003.

12. 'Abdu'l-Bahá, *Promulgation of Universal Peace*, 452.

13. Shoghi Effendi, *This Decisive Hour*, no. 85.11; Bahá'u'lláh, quoted in Shoghi Effendi, *Advent of Divine Justice*, 69.

14. Universal House of Justice, *Messages from the Universal House of Justice, 1963–1986*, 466.

15. Taherzadeh, 1:270.

16. Bahá'u'lláh, *Gleanings*, no. 80.2.

17. Letter written on behalf of Shoghi Effendi, in *Lights of Guidance*, no. 2049.

18. 'Abdu'l-Bahá, *Selections from the Writings of 'Abdu'l-Bahá*, no. 35.12.

19. 'Abdu'l-Bahá, *Selections from the Writings of 'Abdu'l-Bahá*, no. 103.1–6.

20. 'Abdu'l-Bahá, quoted in *The Compilation of Compilations*, 2:1533.

21. 'Abdu'l-Bahá, *Promulgation of Universal Peace*, 63–66.

10 / Life Crises, Trauma, and Growth

The epigraph is from a tablet of 'Abdu'l-Bahá to Charles Haney, May 1911. *Star of the West*, vol. 10, no. 19, 348.

1. Tedeschi and Calhoun, "Posttraumatic Growth," 1, 4.

2. Ibid., 5.

3. Ibid., 5.

4. *Time Magazine,* "The Time 100," www.time.com/time/time100/heroes/profile/keller01.html.

5. Ghadirian, "Psychological and Spiritual Dimensions of Persecution and Suffering," 4; Alexander Herzen, quoted in Hartmann, "Presidential Address," 1135.

6. Frankl, *The Doctor and the Soul,* 121–22.

7. Ghadirian, "Psychological and Spiritual Dimensions of Persecution and Suffering," 4.

8. National Spiritual Assembly of the Bahá'ís of Canada, *Bahá'í Canada,* 10–11; Shoghi Effendi, *Light of Divine Guidance* 1:217; National Spiritual Assembly of the Bahá'ís of Canada, 17.

9. Frankl, *The Doctor and the Soul,* 85.

10. Letters written on behalf of Shoghi Effendi, in *Bahíyyih Khánum,* 83, 75–76.

11. Shoghi Effendi, in *Bahíyyih Khánum,* 35; Khan, *Prophet's Daughter,* 250.

12. Bahíyyih Khánum, in *Bahíyyih Khánum,* 148.

13. Ibid., 139, 145–46, 139.

14. Ghadirian, "Psychological and Spiritual Dimensions of Persecution and Suffering," 11–12.

15. Berger, "Recovery and Regression," 54–59; Ghadirian, "Psychological and Spiritual Dimensions of Persecution and Suffering," 11–12.

16. Ghadirian, "Intergenerational Responses," 516–21.

17. McLeish, "The poet and the press," 44–46; Ghadirian, "Intergenerational Responses," 520–21.

18. Rutter, "Resilience in the Face of Adversity," 599.

19. Ghadirian, "Intergenerational Responses," 519.

20. Stone, *American Psychiatric Glossary,* 97.

21. 'Abdu'l-Bahá, *Promulgation of Universal Peace,* 415; Ghadirian, "Psychological and Spiritual Dimensions of Persecution and Suffering," 4–5.

11 / Spiritual Dimensions of Suffering and Creativity

The epigraph is from a tablet of 'Abdu'l-Bahá to Juliet Thompson in *Star of the West,* vol. 2, nos. 7, 8, and 13.

1. *Compilation of Compilations*, 2:7; Shoghi Effendi, *Bahá'í Administration*, 27; Bahá'u'lláh, in *The Bahá'í Revelation*, 171; Ghadirian, "Psychological and Spiritual Dimensions of Persecution and Suffering," 4; Bahá'u'lláh, *The Seven Valleys and The Four Valleys*, 12.

2. *Newsweek*, June 18, 1984, 57.

3. Frankl, *Man's Search for Meaning*, 178–79.

4. Albert Einstein, cited at http://www.quoteopia.com/famous. php?quotesby=alberteinstein.

5. Ghadirian, "Psychological and Spiritual Dimensions of Persecution and Suffering," 20.

6. Tillich, *Dynamics of Faith*, 2; Ghadirian, "Psychological and Spiritual Dimensions of Persecution and Suffering," 4.

7. Rutter, "Resilience in the Face of Adversity," 598–99.

8. Campbell, quoted in McGowan, "The hidden side of happiness," 74.

9. Ghadirian, "Psychological and Spiritual Dimensions of Persecution and Suffering," 4.

10. Basgoglu et al., "Psychological Effects of Torture," 81.

11. Choy and de Bosset, "Post-traumatic Stress Disorder: An Overview," 579; Ghadirian, "Psychological and Spiritual Dimensions of Persecution and Suffering," 4.

12. 'Abdu'l-Bahá, *'Abdu'l-Bahá in London*, 28.

Conclusion

1. 'Abdu'l-Bahá, *Secret of Divine Civilization*, 2–3.

2. Shoghi Effendi, *World Order of Bahá'u'lláh*, 204.

3. Bahá'u'lláh, The Kitáb-i-Aqdas, ¶33.

4. Pargament et al., "Spirituality: a pathway to posttraumatic growth or decline?" 121–25.

5. Albert Einstein, quoted at http://www.quoteopia.com/famous. php?quotesby=alberteinstein.

6. Letter written on behalf of the Universal House of Justice, *Lights of Guidance*, no. 1228.

Bibliography

WORKS BY BAHÁ'U'LLÁH

The Hidden Words. Wilmette, IL: Bahá'í Publishing, 2002.

Gleanings from the Writings of Bahá'u'lláh. Translated by Shoghi Effendi. Wilmette, IL: Bahá'í Publishing, 2005.

The Seven Valleys and The Four Valleys. Translated by Ali-Kuli Khan and Marzieh Gail. New ed. Wilmette, IL: Bahá'í Publishing Trust, 1991.

WORKS BY 'ABDU'L-BAHÁ

'Abdu'l-Bahá in London: Addresses and Notes of Conversations. London: Bahá'í Publishing Trust, 1982.

Bahá'í World Faith. Wilmette, IL: Bahá'í Publishing Trust, 1976.

Paris Talks: Addresses Given By 'Abdu'l-Bahá in Paris in 1911. Wilmette, IL: Bahá'í Publishing, 2006.

Promulgation of Universal Peace: Talks Delivered by 'Abdu'l-Bahá during His Visit to the United States and Canada in 1912. Compiled by Howard MacNutt. New ed. Wilmette, IL: Bahá'í Publishing Trust, 2007.

The Secret of Divine Civilization. Translated by Marzieh Gail. 1st pocket-sized ed. Wilmette, IL: Bahá'í Publishing Trust, 1990.

Selections from the Writings of 'Abdu'l-Bahá. Compiled by the Research Department of the Universal House of Justice. Translated by a Committee at the Bahá'í World Center and Marzieh Gail. 1st pocket-size ed. Wilmette, IL: Bahá'í Publishing Trust, 1996.

Some Answered Questions. Compiled and translated by Laura Clifford Barney. 1st pocket-size ed. Wilmette, IL: Bahá'í Publishing Trust, 1984.

Tablet to August Forel, in *The Bahá'í World*, 15:37–43.

WORKS BY SHOGHI EFFENDI

Advent of Divine Justice, The. Wilmette, IL: Bahá'í Publishing Trust, 1990.

Arohanui: Letters from Shoghi Effendi to New Zealand. Suva, Fiji: Bahá'í Publishing Trust, 1982.

Bahá'í Administration: Selected Letters 1922–1932. 5th ed. Wilmette, IL: Bahá'í Publishing Trust, 1968.

This Decisive Hour: Messages from Shoghi Effendi to the North American Bahá'ís, 1932–1946. Wilmette, IL: Bahá'í Publishing Trust, 2002.

The Light of Divine Guidance: The Messages from the Guardian of the Bahá'í Faith to the Bahá'ís of Germany and Austria. Hofheim-Langenheim: Bahá'í-Verlag, 1982.

The Unfolding Destiny of the British Bahá'í Community: The Messages of the Guardian of the Bahá'í Faith to the Bahá'ís of the British Isles. London: Bahá'í Publishing Trust, 1981.

The World Order of Bahá'u'lláh. Wilmette, IL: Bahá'í Publishing Trust, 1991.

WORKS BY THE UNIVERSAL HOUSE OF JUSTICE

Messages from the Universal House of Justice, 1963–1985. Wilmette, IL: Bahá'í Publishing Trust, 1986.

Turning Point: Selected Messages of the Universal House of Justice and Supplementary Material, 1996–2006. West Palm Beach, FL: Palabra Publications, 2006.

COMPILATIONS OF BAHÁ'Í WRITINGS

Bahá'u'lláh, the Báb, and 'Abdu'l-Bahá. *The Divine Art of Living: Selections from the Writings of Bahá'u'lláh, the Báb, and 'Abdu'l-Bahá.* Compiled by Mabel Hyde Paine, revised by Anne Marie Scheffer. Wilmette, IL: Bahá'í Publishing, 2006.

Bahá'u'lláh and 'Abdu'l-Bahá. *The Reality of Man.* Compiled by Terry Cassiday, Christopher J. Martin, and Bahhaj Taherzadeh. Wilmette, IL: Bahá'í Publishing, 2005.

Bahá'u'lláh and 'Abdu'l-Bahá. *The Bahá'í Revelation: A Selection from the Bahá'í Holy Writings.* London: Bahá'í Publishing Trust, 1955.

Bahá'u'lláh, the Báb, 'Abdu'l-Bahá, Shoghi Effendi, the Universal House of Justice. *The Compilation of Compilations Prepared by the Universal House of Justice, 1963–1990.* Maryborough, Australia: Bahá'í Publications of Australia, 1991.

Helen Hornby, compiler. *Lights of Guidance.* New ed. New Delhi: Bahá'í
Publishing Trust, 1999.

OTHER WORKS

Adams, J. L. and J. K. Addison. *The Care and Feeding of Ideas: A Guide to
Encouraging Creativity.* Don Mills, Ontario: Wesley Publishing Co., Inc., 1986.

Akinola, Modupe and Betty Mendes. "The dark side of creativity: Biological
vulnerability and negative emotions lead to greater artistic creativity."
Personality and Social Psychology Bulletin 34, no. 12 (2008): 1677–86.

Akiskal, H. and K. Akiskal. "Reassessing the prevalence of bipolar disorders:
clinical significance and artistic creativity." *Psychiatry and Psychobiology* 3:
29s–36s.

Allen, Jon G. *Coping with Trauma: Hope Through Understanding.* American
Psychiatric Press, Inc., 1995.

American News, "The 'Most Miserable Man Alive' Saved a Nation," August
17, 1990.

Andreasen N. C. "Creativity and Mental Illness: Prevalence rates in writers
and their first-degree relatives." *American Journal of Psychiatry* 144, no. 10
(1987): 1288–92.

———. "The diagnosis of schizophrenia." *Schizophrenia Bull* 13 (1987): 9–22.

American Psychiatric Association. *Diagnostic and Statistical Manual of Mental
Disorders.* 3rd ed. Washington, D. C.: American Psychiatric Association,
1980.

APA Online. *Psychology Matters* website. "Turning Lemons into Lemonade:
Hardiness Helps People Turn Stressful Circumstances into Opportunities."
http://www.psychologymatters.org/hardiness.html.

Arehart-Treichel, Joan. "Several factors critical in ability to handle crises."
Psychiatric News. USA edition. (March 3, 2006): 12.

———. "Tchaikovsky turns demons into works of beauty." *Psychiatric News,*
April 19, 2002, 36–37.

———. "Marital strife may keep wounds from healing." *Psychiatric News,*
February 3, 2006, 22.

Bahá'í Canada, October 2005, 10–11.

Basgoglu, M., and M. Metin, Murat Paker, Ozgum Paker, E. Ozman, I.
Marks, C. Inces, D. Sahin, N. Sarimurat. "Psychological Effects of Torture:

A Comparison of Tortured with Nontortured Political Activists in Turkey." *American Journal of Psychiatry* 151 (1994): 76–81.

Beauregard, Mario, and Denyse O'Leary. *The Spiritual Brain: a Neuroscientist's Case for the Existence of the Soul.* New York: HarperOne, 2007.

Beil, Laura. "Using Stress to Heal." *The Montreal Gazette,* September 4, 2004, A21.

Berger, Ann. "Palliative Care in Long-Term-Care Facilities—A Comprehensive Model." *Journal of the American Geriatrics Society* 49, no. 11 (February 7, 2002): 1570–71.

Berger, D. M. "Recovery and Regression in Concentration Camp Survivors: A Psychodynamic Re-evaluation." *Canadian Journal of Psychiatry* 30 (February 1985): 54–59.

Breheny, K. A. *After the Darkest Hour.* New York: Henry Holt & Co., 2000.

Breitbart, W., and K. Heller. "Reframing hope: Meaning-centered care for patients near the end of life." *Journal of Palliative Medicine* 6, no. 6 (2003): 979–88.

Brenner, C. "Creativity and psychodynamics." *Psychoanalytic Quarterly.* LXXIII (2004): 511–15.

Briggs, J. and F. D. Peat. *Turbulent Mirror.* New York: Harper and Row, 1989.

Bryson, Alan. *Healing Mind, Body and Soul.* New Delhi: Sterling Publishers, 1999.

Burns, David. *Feeling Good—The New Mood Therapy.* New York: A Signet Book, 1981.

Çambel, A. B. *Applied Chaos Theory—A Paradigm for Complexity.* San Diego: Academic Press, Inc., 1993.

Calhoun, L. G. and R. G. Tedeschi, eds. *Handbook of Posttraumatic Growth.* New York: Lawrence Erlbaum Associates, 2006.

Cameron, John. "A proposed model of imagination and creativity." *Wisconsin Academy Review* 34, no.3, (June 1988): 33–36.

Campbell, M. and J. Shay. "Pervasive Development Disorders." In *Comprehensive Textbook of Psychiatry,* 6th edition, edited by H. I. Kaplan and B. J. Sadock, 2:2277. Baltimore: William and Wilkins, 1995.

Caplan G. "Mastery of stress: psychological aspects." *American Journal of Psychiatry,* 138 (1981): 413–20.

Cardwell, Mark. "Voyer's voyage." *The Medical Post.* Canadian edition. (October 1, 2002): 29.

Carota, A., G. Iaria, A. Berney, J. Bogousslavsky. *Understanding Van Gogh's Night: Bipolar Disorder.* Vol. 19 of *Neurological Disorder in Famous Artists,* edited by Bogousslavsky J., and F. Boller. New York: Karger, 2005, 121–31.

Cassell, Eric J. "The Nature of Suffering and the Goals of Medicine." *New England Journal of Medicine* 306 (March 1982): 639–45.

———. "The Relief of Suffering." *Archives of Internal Medicine* 143 (1983): 522–23.

Cherry, Laurence. "On the real benefits of eustress." *Psychology Today* 12 (March 1978): 60–70.

Choy, Thomas, and Farideh de Bosset. "Post-traumatic Stress Disorder: An Overview." *Canadian Journal of Psychiatry* 37 (1992): 578–83.

Cousins, Norman. *Anatomy of an Illness.* New York: Bantam Books, 1979.

Coutu, Diane L. "How Resilience Works." *Harvard Business Review* (May 2002): 48.

Crutch, S. J., R. Isaacs, and M. N. Rossor. "Some workmen can blame their tools: artistic change in an individual with Alzheimer's disease." *The Lancet* 357 (June 30, 2001): 2129–2133.

Davidson, Michael W., and the Florida State University. "The Endorphin Collection." http://www.microscopy.fsu.edu/micro/gallery/endorphin/endorphins.html.

Druss, B. G. and S. C. Marcus. "Use of psychotropic medications before and after Sept. 11, 2001." *American Journal of Psychiatry* 161, no. 8 (August, 2004): 1377–83.

DuPont, Robert, M.D. *The Selfish Brain: Learning From Addiction.* Washington, D.C.: American Psychiatric Press, 1997.

Edwards, Steve. "Christopher Reeve: Will of Steel." *The Montreal Gazette,* Oct. 12, 2004, D7.

Eisenman, R. "Creativity, preference for complexity and physical and mental illness." *Creativity Research Journal* 3, no. 3 (1990): 231–36.

Eliade, Mircea, ed. *Encylopedia of Religion.* New York: MacMillan Publishing Co., 1987.

Esslemont, J. E. *Bahá'u'lláh and the New Era: An Introduction to the Bahá'í Faith.* Wilmette, IL: Bahá'í Publishing, 2006.

Faizi, G., ed. *Stories about 'Abdu'l-Bahá.* New Delhi: Bahá'í Publishing Trust, 1981.

Fettes, I. "Migraine Linked to Low Endorphins." *Medical Post* 9, no. 15 (July 26, 1983): 38.

Fitzgerald, M. *Autism and Creativity: Is there a link between autism in men and exceptional ability?* Hove, UK: Brunner-Routledge, 2004.

Fitzgerald, M. and B. O'Brien. *Genius Genes.* Shawnee Mission, Kansas: Autism Asperger Publishing Company, 2007.

Flach, Frederic. "Disorders of the Pathways involved in the Creative Process." *Creativity Research Journal* 3, no. 2 (1990): 158–165.

Frankl, Viktor E. *The Doctor and the Soul.* New York: Bantam Books, 1955.

———. *Man's Search for Meaning.* New York: Simon & Schuster, 1963.

Fromm, Erich. *To Have or To Be?* New York: Harper & Row, 1976.

Frosch, W. A. "Moods, Madness and Music. I. Major Affective Disease and Musical Creativity." *Comprehensive Psychiatry* 28, no. 4 (1987): 316–22.

Ghadirian, Abdu'l-Missagh. "Human responses to life stress and suffering." *The Divine Institution of Marriage, Bahá'í Studies Notebook* 3, nos. 1 and 2 (March 1983): 49–62.

———. "Profile of stress-prone individuals." *Modern medicine of Canada* 39, no. 6 (1984): 673–79.

———. "Psychological and Spiritual Dimensions of Persecution and Suffering." *Journal of Bahá'í Studies* 6, no. 3 (1994).

———. "Intergenerational Responses to the Persecution of the Bahá'ís of Iran." *International Handbook of Multigenerational Legacies of Trauma.* New York: Plenum Press, 1998, pp. 513–32.

Goodwin, D. W. *Alcohol and the Writer.* New York: Ballantine Books, 1988.

Goodwin, F. K. and K. R. Jamison. "Manic Depressive Illness and Creativity, and Leadership" in *Manic Depressive Illness.* New York: Oxford University Press, 1990.

Hartmann, L. "Presidential Address." *American Journal of Psychiatry* 149, no. 9 (September 1992):1135.

Helwig, David. "Physician-poet intrigued by the psychopathology of creative minds." *Can Med Assoc Journal* 142, no. 6 (1990): 650–53.

Jamer, Roderick. "An incurable affliction—Beethoven's twin genius for sublime music and suffering." http://groups.msn.com/SARCOIDOSISDISEASE/general.msnw?action=get_message&mview=0&ID_Message=302&LastModified=4675526464833837699.

Jamison K. R. "Mood disorders and patterns of creativity in British writers and artists." *Psychiatry* 52 (1989): 125–34.

———. *Touched with Fire: Manic Depressive Illness and the Artistic Temperament.* New York: The Free Press, 1993.

———. "Manic depressive illness and creativity," *Scientific American*, February, 1995, 62–67.

———. Manic-Depressive Illness, Genes and Creativity in Genetics and Mental Illness. Edited by L. L. Hall. New York: Plenum Press, 1996.

Miller, B.L cited by Jeffrey, S. "How some declining dementia patients gain creative abilities." *The Medical Post.* Canadian edition. (September 14, 1998): 46.

Jennings, Shawn. *Locked In Locked Out.* Saint John, NB: Dreamcatcher Publishing, 2002.

Kasi, Meana. "Creativity and Depression." *Verge Magazine* 1, no. 5 (December 2000).

Khan, Janet A. *Prophet's Daughter.* Wilmette, IL: Bahá'í Publishing, 2005.

Khavari, K. A. *Spiritual Intelligence.* New Liskeard, Ont: White Mountain Publications, 2000.

Kiecolt-Glaser, Janice K., Timothy J. Loving, Jeffrey R. Stowell, William B. Malarkey, Stanley Lemeshow, Stephanie L. Dickinson, Ronald Glaser. "Hostile Marital Interactions, Proinflammatory Cytokine Production, and Wound Healing." *Archives of General Psychiatry* 62 (2005): 1377–84.

Kim-Cohen, J., T. E. Moffitt, A. Caspi, A. Taylor. "Genetic and environmental processes in young children's resilience and vulnerability to socioeconomic deprivation." *Child Development* 75, no. 3 (May / June 2004): 651–68.

Kluger, J. "He Never Gave Up." *Time Magazine*, October 25, 2004, 53.

Koenig, H. G., M. E. McCullough, D. B. Larson. *Handbook of Religion and Health.* New York: Oxford University Press, 2001.

Krieger, Richard Alan. *Civilization's Quotations.* New York: Algora Publishing, 2002.

Kubler-Ross, Elizabeth. *Death—the Final Stage of Growth.* Inglewood Cliffs, NJ: Prentice-Hall, Inc., 1975.

Lample, Paul. *Creating a New Mind.* Riviera Beach, FL: Palabra Publications, 1999.

Lazarus, R. S., and S. Folman. *Stress, Appraisal and Coping.* New York: Springer Publishing Company, 1984.

Leicester, John. "Cancer survivor wins top cycling prize for unprecedented sixth time," *The Montreal Gazette*, July 26, 2004, A1 and A4.

Levin, A. "Some find silver lining in hurricane clouds." *Psychiatric News*, October 8, 2006, 10.

Levitin D. J., K. Cole, M. Chiles, Z. Lai, A. Lincoln, U. Bellugi. "Characterizing the musical phenotype in individuals with Williams Syndrome." *Child Neuropsychology* 10, no. 4: 223–47.

Lipowski Z. L. "Psychiatry: Mindless or Brainless, Both or Neither." *Canadian Journal of Psychiatry* 34 (April 1989): 249.

Long, Marion, and Jerri Nielson. *Psychology Today*, March / April 2006, 75.

MacLeish, A. "The poet and the press," *Atlantic Monthly*, 44–46.

Maddi, S. R. "Hardiness training at Illinois Bell Telephone." In *Health Promotion Evaluation*, edited by J. P. Opatz. Stevens Point, WI: National Wellness Institute, 1987, 101–15.

McGowan, Kathleen. "The hidden side of happiness," *Psychology Today*, March / April 2006, 70.

Mell, J. C., S. M. Howard, B. L. Miller. "Art and the Brain: The influence of frontotemporal dementia on an accomplished artist." *Neurology* 60 (March 2003): 1707–10.

Miller B. L, M. Ponton, D. F. Benson, J. L. Cummings, I. Mena. "Enhanced artistic creativity with temporal lobe degeneration." *Lancet* 348 (1996): 1744–55.

Miller, B. L., J. Cummings, F. Mishkin, K. Boone, F. Prince, M. Ponton, C. Cotman. "Emergence of artistic talent in frontotemporal dementia." *Neurology* 51, no. 4 (Oct. 1, 1998): 978–82.

Miller, B. L., K. Boone, J. L. Cumming, S. L. Read, F. Mishkin. "Functional correlates of musical and visual ability in frontotemporal dementia." *British Journal of Psychiatry* 176 (2000): 458–63.

Milton, John. *Paradise Lost*, Book 1, lines 254–55, cited in *The Columbia World of Quotations*, edited by Robert Andrews, Mary Biggs, and Michael Seidel. New York: Columbia University Press, 1996.

Mohammadreza, Hojat. *Empathy in Patient Care*. New York: Springer, 2007.

Moran, Lord C. M. W. *Winston Churchill: The Struggle for Survival, 1940–1965: Taken from the Diaries of Lord Moran*. Boston: Houghton Mifflin, 1966.

Moskavitz S. "Longitudinal follow-up of child survivors of the Holocaust." *Journal of American Academy of Child and Adolescent Psychiatry* 24 (1985): 401–7.

Mount, B. M., W. Lawlor, E. J. Cassel. "Spirituality and health: developing a shared vocabulary." *Annals RCPSC* 35, no. 5 (2002): 303–8.

Nash, Alana. "Going the Distance." *Reader's Digest,* December 2004, 67–73.

National Spiritual Assembly of the Bahá'ís of Canada. *Bahá'í Canada,* January 2000, 17.

Neihart, Maureen. "Creativity, the Arts and Madness." *Roeper Review* 21, no. 1 (1998): 47–50.

New Zealand Bahá'í News. "Spiritual education of children: Accustom children to hardship so that they are equipped for trials of life," Sept/Oct. 2000, 1.

Newsweek. (Section on International—Iran) June 18, 1984, 57.

Pargament, Kenneth I., Kavita M. Desai, and Kelly M. McConnell. "Spirituality: a pathway to posttraumatic growth or decline?" in *Handbook of Postttraumatic Growth Research and Practice,* edited by Lawrence G. Calhoun and Richard G. Tedeschi. New York: Lawrence Erlbaum Associates, 2006.

Pettigrew, Eileen. "I believe in miracles." *Reader's Digest,* March 1981, 52.

Post, Felix. "Creativity and psychopathology: A study of 291 world-famous men." *British Journal of Psychiatry* 165 (1994): 22–34.

Rees, W Linford. "Stress, distress and disease." *British Journal of Psychiatry* 128 (1976) 3.

Research Department at the Bahá'í World Center, comp. *Bahiyyih Khanum.* Haifa: Bahá'í World Center, 1982.

Richards, R. and D. K. Kinney. "Mood Swings and Creativity." *Creativity Research Journal* 3, no. 3 (1990): 202–17.

Richards, R., D. K. Kinney, I. Lunde, M. Benet, APC Merzel. "Creativity in manic-depressives, cyclothymes, their normal relatives and control subjects." *Journal of Abnormal Psychology* 97 (1988): 281–88.

Rosenthal, N. E. *Seasons of the Mind.* New York: Bantam Books, 1989.

Rossetti, A. O. and J. Bogousslavsky. "Dostoevsky and Epilepsy: An Attempt to Look through the Frame." Vol. 19 of *Neurological Disorders in Famous Artists,* edited by J. Bogousslavsky and F. Boller. Basel: Karger, 2005, 65–75.

Rothenberg, Albert. "Bipolar illness, creativity, and treatment." *Psychiatric Quarterly* 72 (November 2, 2001): 133–34.

Rutter, Michael. "Resilience in the Face of Adversity: Protective factors and resistance to psychiatric disorder." *British Journal of Psychiatry* 147 (1985): 598–611.

Schuckit, M. A. "Creativity." *Drug Abuse and Alcoholism Newsletter* 19, no. 6 (1990): 1–2.

Segal, J. and M. Weinfeld. "Do children cope better than adults with potentially traumatic stress? A 40-year follow-up of Holocaust survivors." *Psychiatry* 64, no. 1 (Spring 2001): 69.

Selye, Hans. *Stress Without Distress.* Scarborough, Ontario: A New American Library of Canada Ltd., 1974.

Shriqui, Christian. "Schizophrenia and the Heart of Creation." *Psychiatric News* (May 6, 1994): 12.

Siebert, Al. *The Resiliency Advantage.* San Francisco: Berrett-Koehler Publishers, Inc., 2005.

Simeonova, Diana, Kiki Chang, Connie Strong, and Terence Ketter. "Creativity in familial bipolar disorder." *Journal of Psychiatric Research* 39, no. 6 (November 2005): 623–31.

Springer, S. P. and G. Deutsch. *Left Brain, Right Brain.* New York: W. H. Freeman and Company, 1989.

Star of the West. Vol. 2, nos. 7 and 8, 13.

———. Vol. 10, no. 19, 348.

———. Vol. 14, no. 2, 41.

Stewart, Ian. *Does God play dice? The New Mathematics of Chaos.* 2nd ed. Malden, MA: Blackwell, 2002.

Stone, E. M. *American Psychiatric Glossary.* 6th ed. Washington, DC: American Psychiatric Press, 1988.

Storr, A. *Churchill's Black Dog, Kafka's Mice, and Other Phenomena of the Human Mind.* New York: Grove Press, 1988.

———. "Solitude." In M. Fitzgerald and B. O'Brien, *Genius Genes.* Shawnee Mission, KA: Autism Asperger Publishing Company, 2007.

Taherzadeh, Adib. *The Revelation of Bahá'u'lláh: Baghdád 1853–63.* Oxford: George Ronald, 1976.

Targ, Elizabeth. "Research methodology for studies of prayer and distant healing." *Complementary Therapies in Nursing and Midwifery,* 8 (2002): 29–41.

Taylor, R. *Robert Schumann: His Life and Work.* London: Granada, 1982.

Tchaikovsky, P. I. *The Life and Letters of Peter Ilyich Tchaikovsky.* Edited and translated by R. Newmarch. London: John Lane, 1906.

Tedeschi R. G. and L. G. Calhoun. "Posttraumatic growth: conceptual foundation and empirical evidence." *Psychological Inquiry* 15, no. 1 (2004): 1–18.

Tillich, Paul. *Dynamics of Faith*. New York: Harper and Row, 1957.

The Time 100. Year 2000. www.time.com/time/time100/heroes/profile/keller01.html.

Treffert, D. A. and G. L. Wallace. "Islands of Genius." *Scientific American*, June 2002, 78–80.

Tryk, H. E. "Assessment in the study of creativity" in *Advances in Psychological Assessments*, vol. 1, edited by P. McReynolds. Palo Alto: Science of Behavior Books, 1970.

Warner, E. "The role of belief in healing." *Canadian Medical Association Journal* 128 (1983): 1108.

Williams, Nigel. "Abstract." *Current Biology* 13, no. 11 (January 8, 2003): R3–R4.

Wolfe, M. S. "Shutting down Alzheimer's." *Scientific American*, May 2006, 73.

Woolf, V. *The Letters of Virginia Woolf.* 6 vols. Edited by N. Nicholson and J. Trautman. New York: Harcourt, 1975–1980.

Yazdani, Farhan. "La dimension spirituelle des relations mere-enfant." *Actes de la VIIème journée d'étude de l'Association médicale Bahá'íe*, 1993.

Zausner, Tobi. "When walls become doorways: creativity, chaos theory and physical illness." *Creativity Research Journal* 11, no. 1 (1998): 21–28.

Index

Index

Bahá'í
PUBLISHING
and the Bahá'í Faith

Bahá'í Publishing produces books based on the teachings of the Bahá'í Faith. Founded over 160 years ago, the Bahá'í Faith has spread to some 235 nations and territories and is now accepted by more than five million people. The word "Bahá'í" means "follower of Bahá'u'lláh." Bahá'u'lláh, the founder of the Bahá'í Faith, asserted that He is the Messenger of God for all of humanity in this day. The cornerstone of His teachings is the establishment of the spiritual unity of humankind, which will be achieved by personal transformation and the application of clearly identified spiritual principles. Bahá'ís also believe that there is but one religion and that all the Messengers of God—among them Abraham, Zoroaster, Moses, Krishna, Buddha, Jesus, and Muḥammad—have progressively revealed its nature. Together, the world's great religions are expressions of a single, unfolding divine plan. Human beings, not God's Messengers, are the source of religious divisions, prejudices, and hatreds.

The Bahá'í Faith is not a sect or denomination of another religion, nor is it a cult or a social movement. Rather, it is a globally recognized independent world religion founded on new books of scripture revealed by Bahá'u'lláh.

Bahá'í Publishing is an imprint of the National Spiritual Assembly of the Bahá'ís of the United States.

For more information about the Bahá'í Faith,
or to contact Bahá'ís near you, visit
http://www.bahai.us/
or call
1-800-22-unite

Other Books Available
from Bahá'í Publishing

High Desert
A Journey of Survival and Hope
KIM DOUGLAS
$20.00 U.S. / $22.00 CAN
Trade Paper
ISBN 978-1-931847-59-9

A deeply moving memoir with a holistic approach to overcoming the effects of growing up in a severely abusive home

High Desert is a courageous, gripping, and deeply personal autobiographical account about growing up in an abusive home and finding a path to recovery by learning to rely on faith and spiritual beliefs to heal and grow in ways that go beyond traditional twelve-step programs and other approaches. In this eye-opening account, Kim Douglas reveals a wide range of issues and behaviors that will be familiar to many who have come from similar circumstances: eating disorders, obsessive or compulsive behaviors, and troubled relationships with friends and family members. Most important is the author's insight and experience in finding effective ways of coping with life's challenges, learning to trust others in a close relationship, parenting without repeating the cycle of abuse, healing the relationship with the abuser, and forgiving those who don't help in a time of crisis.

Illumine My Family
Prayers and Meditations from the Bahá'í Faith
BAHÁ'U'LLÁH, THE BÁB, AND 'ABDU'L-BAHÁ
Compiled by Bahá'í Publishing
$12.00 U.S. / $13.50 CAN
Trade Paper
ISBN 978-1-931847-62-9

A heartwarming collection of prayers for people of all faiths to meet the challenges of everyday life

Illumine My Family is a collection of prayers and meditative passages from the writings of the Bahá'í Faith that will help any family wishing to incorporate spirituality into their daily lives. The passages included offer guidance and prayers on subjects relevant to any family regardless of their background or current circumstances. Subjects covered include marriage, parents, motherhood, children, love, healing, the loss of a loved one, and more. The book has been put together with the hope that it will assist families to grow together and to foster strong relationships with each other and with God.

Life at First Sight
Finding the Divine in the Details
PHYLLIS EDGERLY RING
$15.00 U.S. / $17.00 CAN
Trade Paper
ISBN 978-1-931847-67-4

Phyllis Ring divulges in this collection of personal essays how to "see the spiritual" in everyday moments and everyday life. Like love at first sight, "life at first sight" focuses on instant recognition and irresistible attraction, a sense of something mysteriously familiar and a sense of spiritual connection. The essays show how to develop a new sense of being during daily activities and everyday interactions, as well as through engagement with the natural world. As a jumping-off point for spiritual conversation, these compositions offer food for thought on how to lead a more spiritual life.

". . . Captures the web of meaning that unites and sustains all of human life. These sparkling essays remind us that the spiritual side of life is not a luxury or an optional nicety, but utterly crucial. At this moment in history, no message is more vital."—**Larry Dossey, MD, Author of** *The Power of Premonitions* **and** *The Extraordinary Healing Power of Ordinary Things*

"These essays are a treasure, especially as they pursue the journey of the human spirit through the perils—and joys—of 'the road not taken.' This is the sort of book that will warm, celebrate, and console the reader on a sour day. The book is lovingly written and beautifully conceived, and dares to approach the practical reality of the spiritual life."—**Dolores Kendrick, Poet Laureate of the District of Columbia and Author of** *Why the Woman Is Singing on the Corner* **and** *Now Is the Thing to Praise*

The Universe Within Us
A Guide to the Purpose of Life
JANE E. HARPER
$15.00 U.S. / $17.00 CAN
Trade Paper
ISBN 978-1-931847-58-2

A provocative look at the purpose of life through a mixture of religion, science, and personal experience

Author Jane E. Harper offers insight into a new way to look at life. *The Universe Within Us* is a mixture of science, religion, and personal experience that offers a new understanding of our place and purpose in the universe—an understanding that leads to the conclusion that every human being possesses a spiritual nature. Harper argues that, traditionally, answers to questions about the purpose of life have long been the domain of priests and clergy, and, more recently, scientists—and often the answers have been less than satisfying. The religious answers often leave the intellect out and defy what the rational mind can accept, while the scientific answers satisfy the intellect at the expense of the heart and soul. Drawing on resources available from the sciences, from the world's sacred scriptures, and from personal observations and experiences, she offers a unique map of the universe and an explanation of life's purpose that is truly satisfying.

To view our complete catalog,
Please visit http://books.bahai.us